CW01664282

21 DA
IMITATING
CHRIST

GILES STEVENS

21 Days of Imitating Christ

Copyright 2013 by Giles Stevens

All rights reserved

No part of this book may be reproduced or transmitted in any form or by any means, electronic or mechanical, including photocopying, recording, or by any information storage and retrieval system, without permission in writing from the author.

Edited and published by: Giles Stevens

Email: admin@vinechurch.co.uk

Website: www.vinechurch.co.uk

21 DAYS IMITATING CHRIST

GILES STEVENS

Giles Stevens and his wife Silvia pastor Vine Church UK – an international cell church based in the city of Swindon, UK. Previously he worked as an evangelist in Asia and South America.

The broader network, Vine Church International, is becoming known worldwide as a place where "every member is a minister" and for its vision of building churches of "overcomers".

Giles' first book "The 11th Question – the spiritual self-analysis test" became an instant best seller. Other books now include; Winning Your World, 21 days to Refresh Your Relationships and Joshua's Journey.

Contact: admin@vinechurch.co.uk

Tel: 01793 862224

Contents

A Time of Imitating Christ

Imitate me, just as I also imitate Christ.
(1 Corinthians 11.1)

We tend to think of imitations in a negative light; as cheaper or inferior copies of the original. We also tend to think of imitations in worldly terms. Those in business will remember how the Japanese became the great imitators of American products in the post-war period and built up their industry by producing copies of the American counterparts at much lower prices. Imitation also conjures up imagines of school boys making fun of one anther or as a way for weak people to find their own identity by copying others. We wear the fashion labels or drink the same drinks as those we want to impress or appear like.

Yet Paul's oft-overlooked words to the church at Corinth are vitally relevant to us today if we are to understand the call of God to be Christ-like and the purpose of God to make disciples. Imitating God is actually mentioned three times in the New Testament stressing the importance of it (Eph 5.1, 3 Jn 1.11, 1Cor 11.1). Imitation of men of God is also encouraged (Heb 6.12, 1Co 4.16) Clearly imitation can be a very positive thing and need not be interpreted negatively. After all we are called to be imitators not only of good but of God Himself. As we imitate Him we become like Him. Jesus is the expressed image of God (Heb 1.3). In being so He is the divine model for us to emulate.

The Model

The more of Christ's likeness we have, the more of His influence we have. The more of His influence, the more the world around us is shaped into His will; His Kingdom comes and His will is done on earth as it is in heaven.

So what does Paul mean by becoming imitators? Let us avoid all religiosity immediately and remember that Paul lived and died to show that we are not to follow rules and regulations but rather to develop our relationship with God. The great desire of his heart was "to know Him, and the power of His resurrection and the fellowship of His sufferings' (Phil 3.10). His desire therefore that we are imitators not so much in external things or appearance but rather in the things of the heart, in the patterns of mind, in our attitudes and our actions. His exhortation is not that we wear the same type of clothing or eat the same type of food. We do not need to put on "Jesus sandals", grow beards and wear lose clothing! Paul never expected Gentiles to become Jews. Rather he positively fought against such Judaizing opinions of his day (Gal 5.1). His imitation of Christ was to be one an imitation of the heart. His advice to the gentiles was not physical circumcision but circumcision of the heart (Rom 2.29).

The purpose of this fast is that we spend the month really seeking to be like Christ in thought, attitude and lifestyle. We must become like Him. Hence we must hold up the mirror of God's word to our lives everyday and reject and change anything that does not match thc divine original.

The Material

To imitate a product you must consider the original parts and then built exact replicas using the best quality materials. We need not fear that we are of inferior quality. Incredible as it may seem the fact of the matter remains that we are made of the same stuff as our heavenly counterpart. In the beginning man was made in "God's image and likeness". Psalm 8.5 states that man is made a little lower than Elohim (God Himself) and the Apostle John exultantly says; "As He is, so are we in this world"(1 John 4.17). It is true that we have yet to receive our heavenly bodies but at the same time Scripture is clear that we have "received all things that pertain to godliness" (2 Pet 1.3) and that we have "received every spiritual blessing in heavenly places" (Eph 1.3).

The Means

In addition to having the right model to copy and the right materials to work with we also have means of achieving such an end. The work of the Holy Spirit is to build into the believer the character of Christ. He is the one that transforms us "into the same image, from glory to glory". (2Cor 3.18). Now this is everything. Here we discover that it is not only God's desire that we become like Him (and His desires shall come to pass) but also God has made available His power in order for the job to be completed. After all this is no work within man's capability. You are not able to change the deep things of the heart yourself anymore than a man can jump over the moon. This requires divine intervention and help. Thankfully this is on offer and as we humble ourselves in prayer and ask God to change us, His mighty hand comes down and works deeply within. He is the potter and we are the clay. He is the alchemist and we are the gold. We must do our part in seeking Him with all of our hearts. But we can rest assured that God answers the prayers of the righteous. If we draw near to

Him, He will draw near to us and make the changes that we both want and need.

THE MAN

The disciples were Christ's imitators. The religious leaders perceived that these unlearned men had been with Jesus (Acts 4.13). The disciples were called Christians at Antioch because they began to think, speak and act like Him (Acts 11.26). They laid their lives down in like manner of their Master.

But how can we imitate Jesus if we cannot see Him? Obviously we can read the Scriptures and learn His ways and we can follow the leading of His Spirit within us. Why then does Paul tell the Corinthians to imitate him as he imitated Christ? Paul was a man who model authentic faith and carried the marks of Christ, not stigmata as some believe, but rather he had been fashioned into the mold of Christ by deep in-workings of the Spirit and outward circumstances and situations. He was not a fashion model but a faith model for his generation. He was flesh and bone that his own team could copy just as the twelve copied Christ.

Paul's spiritual sons, such as Timothy and Titus, were his imitators (and by being so were imitators of Christ). They carried his vision and values. They patterned his lifestyle. Sons tend to like things that their fathers like. We have a young generation of football enthusiasts because their father loved the game.

The Lord will put into your life people who you should look up to as role models. Likewise He will put in your life people who look to you as their model. In our church we call the former disciplers and the latter disciples. In this way Christ's image in stamped upon each generation. Just as God used the man Christ Jesus to form the first group of believers so He uses man today, filled with the same Spirit, to form the next generation of believers.

Some say that they do not need to imitate men, but they deceive themselves. They say they will learn from God alone, not recognizing that most teaching is given to us through men filled with the Spirit. They say that they would love the God that they cannot see but don't love the brother that they can see. Paul was the human model for Timothy. Timothy became the model for others. God is the God of Abraham, Isaac, and Jacob. Abraham modeled faith for Isaac and he in turn model faith for Jacob. Imitation is an intergenerational process.

There are some who think it is a sign of weakness to model yourself on someone else. They think that they must be originators of all things. These people have an "Adam" complex. They think that everything must start with them. But there is nothing new under the sun (Ecc 1.9). We should find that which of Christ and imitate it.

Each day of this campaign we are to consider different characteristics of Christ and to purposefully ask God to build such into our lives. I encourage you to be very intentional about this. As we look at the priorities, patterns and principles of Jesus' lifestyle be sure to make changes in your own life where these are not synchronized. Our intention is to please God in the first place. He will be pleased when we live as He lived. Secondly our intention is to have His influence in our generation. That is the only thing that will change it. The Kingdom will come if the kings live like the King of kings! Yes our desire is to make disciples, multiply cell groups and conquer our generation for Christ. Such heavenly influence comes through the image of the heavenly man in us.

Praying as Christ Prayed

Now in the morning, having risen a long while before daylight, He went out and departed to a solitary place; and there He prayed.
(Mark 1.35)

It took a while for the realisation to dawn on His disciples, but eventually they concluded that Christ's power and wisdom came from a heavenly source. They realised that His public ministry was an expression of His private intimacy with God. They began to see that He was speaking what He had heard His Father say and He was doing what His Father asked Him to do. Hence they approached Him and said; "Master, teach us how to pray" (Luke 11.1).

If we want the same heavenly outpouring we must go to the same heavenly font. This is the starting point for all ministry. Christ spent 40 days praying in the wilderness before He began to preach and do miracles. His disciples spent 10 days praying in the upper room before they began to preach and do miracles. The battles they won in the heavens were then played out on earth.

Hence it is our starting point too. We are to pray as Christ prayed. If we did everything else right and got this wrong, we would fail. Why? Because to pray is to depend on God and upon His arm of strength. Not to pray is to depend on ourselves, which is both vanity and a sure road to disaster. But we are desperate for a move of God. Brothers and sisters, we need to pray like Christ prayed.

Let's consider then how Christ prayed

1. Frequency of prayer

Jesus prayed a lot. His custom was to pray early each morning and He prayed for forty days before starting His ministry (Luke 4.2). We also read that He prayed all night at times. He prayed before eating, before doing miracles, before great trials and in thanksgiving to great victories (Luke 10.21). He seemed to be holding a permanent conversation with His heavenly Father. How wonderful! How comforting!

In like manner, Paul, His imitator, prayed much. We read that that he prayed on ships, beaches, palaces and prisons. He constantly bowed his knees daily to intercede for the fledgling church (Eph 3.14, Rom 1.9). He prayed and saw the Lord respond. No wonder he encourages us to pray unceasingly (ITh 5.17).

Now lets be honest and go to work here. What about us? Is it time to put away our excuses of tiredness and lack of time and begin to put this first in our day? Is prayer a daily custom for us? If we want to receive our daily bread, should we not be saying our daily prayers? Have we not yet perceived that the first thing that is dropped from a busy schedule is our prayer time? Let's make a change in that today. Let's start afresh… in prayer. Let's pray that we are able to pray! Let's start a heavenly dialogue today, both verbalised and silent, that never stops. Let's pray in our cars, in our homes, in our jobs, as we walk down the street, when we visit your friends. Let's offer to pray for people we meet. Let's fill this month with more prayer than we have ever prayed before.

2. Fervency of prayer

Now there seems to be two types of prayer – passionate heart-felt prayers and dry religious prayers. James 5.16 tells us that the effective fervent prayer of the righteous man avails much. In other words, these prayers release power and get heaven's blessing. In contrast, there are vain repetitions spoken from religious lips like a mantra to deceiving spirits (Matt 6.7). God rejects this type of prayer. Jesus prayed fervently. In Gethsemane we find Him sweating drops of blood in prayer; in the temple we see Him driving out the moneychangers who had changed His Father's house of prayer into a den of iniquity.

His imitator Paul modeled this manner. In the prison of Ephesus we find him and his disciple Silas praying with such fervency that the whole prison heard them. He speaks of groanings and utterances in prayer that come through deep and passionate intercession (Rom 8.26).

So here is the question: how fervent are your prayers? Do you lift the roof with the volume or do you barely make a sound? Lions roar but mice squeak! It is possible to pray without your mouth being engaged, but at every chance that you can make a noise you should. Christ verbalised His prayers. You will find that your fervency and focus increase when you are praying aloud. There is power in the spoken word both in the material realm and the spiritual realm. Somebody once said, "But God is not deaf!" Another said, "But He knows what I am thinking!" These have missed the point. We don't life our voices so God can hear us but so our hearts our fully engaged and so that principalities of resistance are bound and heavenly answers come through.

3. Faith-filled prayer

Some of the most marvelous words that fell from Jesus' lips were uttered at the tomb of Lazarus. "Father, I thank You that You have heard Me. And I know that You always hear Me..."(Luke 11.41). Jesus' prayers reflect that fact that He had no shadow of a doubt that God was listening and would answer. He knew of His Father's proximity and His faithfulness. He therefore wanted to instill such confidence and trust in His disciples. For assuredly, I say to you, whoever says to this mountain, 'Be removed and be cast into the sea,' and does not doubt in his heart, but believes that those things he says will be done, he will have whatever he says. Therefore I say to you, whatever things you ask when you pray, believe that you receive them, and you will have them. (Mark 11.23-24)

Paul models this too. He trusts in the power of the name of Jesus. His prayers and declarations are infused with faith. In Lystra he heals a lame man in Jesus' name (Acts 14.10). In Ephesus he delivers a possessed girl in Jesus' name (Acts 16.16). Later in Troas he raised the dead by the same power (Acts 20.12). No wonder he spends time in prayer. He knows that God hears and answers the prayers of the righteous.

It is the prayer of faith that moves mountains. To have faith is to believe in God's promise before it is possible to see the answer in the physical realm. To have faith is make a claim upon that which Christ won for mankind at Calvary. What is now our inheritance on legal terms is made manifest on vital terms by the appropriation of faith. Imagine a relation left you a piece of land in his or her will. To make a claim on that, you need more than a piece of paper in hand. You must take that paper to the land agency and make a claim to it. So to with God's promises. They need to be acted upon.

We need to pray frequently and fervently but also in faith. Believe when you pray for your family and friends that they will be saved. Have faith that they will come to the encounter weekend and pray for them and then invite them. Pray with faith that God is going to bless all that you put your hand to this month, then get up and go for it.

4. Focus of prayer

The Lord was very specific in His prayers. He prayed always the will of God, for He sought that always before He prayed for anything else. He had prayed all night for His Father to reveal to Him who were to be His 12 disciples. (Luk 6.12). In Gethsemane He uttered the immortal words "not as I will, but as You will." (Luk 26.39). Having discovered the will of God, He was most specific in His prayers. He prayed for Peter to return after he was sifted by Satan. This then happened. He prayed for his disciples to be one as He and His Father were one. This happened. At Pentecost they were all with one accord in one place. When prayer is focused, it has power.

Paul prayed for open doors and got them (Col 4.3, 1Co 16.9). He prayed for boldness and became as courageous as a lion (Eph 6.19). He gave birth to the early churches through prayer (Gal 4.19).

The focus of our prayers must always be the glory of God and the advancement of His Kingdom. Within this we must be focused and specific about our prayers. The Lord knows our desires and sees our needs and yet He waits to be ask before He responds.

Where there is focus there is fire. 120 disciples gathered in the upper room in Jerusalem after Christ's ascension to await the promise of the Father. They continued in prayer, focused prayer. They were knowledgeable of the promise of God and therefore prayed for the gift of the Holy Spirit until He arrived. As little boys with magnifying glasses know, if you focus sunlight in one spot it can create fire.

Loving as Jesus Loved

That Christ may dwell in your hearts through faith;
that you, being rooted and grounded in love,
may be able to comprehend with all the saints what is the
width and length and depth and height— to know the love
of Christ which passes knowledge; that you may be filled
with all the fullness of God.
(Eph 3.17-19)

To know God is to know Love. It is His love towards us that conquers our hearts. The bible explains that we only love Him because He loved us first (1Jn 4:19). We don't know real love until we have experienced His love. You cannot give what you have not received. The world is starved of this love. It knows only a sensual type of love. This may conquer the emotions or the mind for a time, but only God's love conquers the heart.

People do not convert simply because they have heard a great message, but because they have experienced, at some level, the love of God in Christ. This is real love stated in a fact: that Christ died for us even when we were sinners (Rom 5:8). But also it is something to be experienced. "Taste and see that the Lord is good" (Psa 34:8). We encounter the Love of God in the Holy

Spirit. He is a Spirit of love. One touch of this and our lives are never the same again. The world will remain the same until this love is "shared around" or "spread abroad" (Rom 5:5). It will melt the hardest heart.

Christ's life is one of total love. His motive was always Love. Sadly human motives, even in church work, can be polluted. Our help of others can be with the selfish motives, such as the applause of man or out of a self-righteous spirit.

When the world comes across a love that is pure and undefiled and selfless, it will surrender to it. This type of love is irresistible to the majority. If only we can love like Jesus loved we will create a generation of Jesus lovers, just as in times past.

Let us consider the characteristics of Jesus' love:

1. The width of Christ's love speaks of His love being universal.

Christ is not just the Saviour of the Jew but also of the Gentile. His love is for every tribe, every nation and every tongue. His arms on the cross were stretched out and nailed down like signposts to the East and to the West. So too His arms of love reach around the world and embrace every nation on the globe. So too did He reach into generations past and generations present and put upon Himself the sin of all humanity as an expression of His divine love. In short He was and is the lover of all (John 3.16).

- **His love transcends nationality – He loved the Jew Matthew and the Samaritan woman at the well.**

- **His love transcends social position – He loved Nicodemus, the temple leader and Bartimaeus the street beggar.**

• His love transcends economic status – He loved the rich young ruler and the widow who had two mites.

• His love transcends age – He loved both the old lady who had been bound for 30 years and the young children.

What about us? Do we love just a certain age group, social bracket, nationality or type of person? Do we look beyond the external man and have compassion on all? People tend to love others who are similar to them. This is not altruistic love but selfish – for by doing it they are loving themselves!

We must spread the life of God to all. Our church must feel like home for old and young, rich and poor, black and white, the strong and the weak. With the Holy Spirit sprinkled upon us, then we have diversity in unity. What a joy to be in such an environment!

2. The length of Christ's love speaks of His love being eternal.

The love of Christ goes from generation to generation. It was from the beginning and it will be there at the end. The Lord never stops loving us. Don't let the devil deceive you into thinking that God withdraws His love when you make a mistake. God's love is steadfast. He loves you in your mistakes. The Father of the prodigal kept loving his son even when his son left him for the world. It was the knowledge of his father's steadfast love that motivated that young man to head home from the pigsty. He knew his father would not reject him.

What about us? Do we love people when they are behaving well and agreeing with us or do we love people no matter what? Do we love because people deserve to be loved or do we love because we are lovers? Jesus loves us because He is love.

3. The depth of Christ's love speaks of His love being unfathomable.

Jesus's love was both for the temple leader Nicodemus but also for the criminal on the cross. His blood was shed for all the sins of the world including the worst of all.

He loves the thief and murderer. He loved the adulteress and the prostitute. Do we love this type of people? His love reaches the depths of hell, those who committed terrible sins. He is not solely the Savior of educated and polite people. He is the savior of terrible criminals? Some of the best saints were terrible sinners. Why? Because they understand the mercy and grace of God better than others. They live a life of gratitude. Those who are forgiven much, love much.

Most criminals have suffered themselves from a lack of love in their lives. I have discovered that hurt people hurt people. Their hearts are wounded and thereby unresponsive at first. But little by little love can conquer them and heal them. The good news is that healed people then go on and heal other people.

4. The height of Christ's love speaks of His love being heavenly.

Man's love is limited. God's love comes from the heights of heaven. His love is a mountain that towers over us. His love is seen principally on the heights of Mount Calvary shed down onto Jerusalem below.

Man's loves on a contractual basis, God loves on a covenant basis. People stop loving if their love is not returned. But God keeps loving us no matter the cost. Man's love is conditional; God's love is unconditional. Man's love is selfish, but God's love is selfless and self-sacrificing. Man's love is earthly; God's love is heavenly.

Therefore man's love is limited, but God's love cuts to the deepest part of the heart. Man's love is superficial, but God's love conquers our hearts. If we were only to practice this altruistic, giving, self-sacrificing heavenly love, the world around us would be quickly won over to Christ.

Fasting as Jesus fasted

"… give yourselves to fasting and prayer…"
(1 Cor 7.5)

Now here we have a subject that is little discussed or taught in Western churches. This is partly because we have not appreciated the power that comes through fasting and partly because we dread the thought of going without food. For many of us the voice of our stomachs has become louder than the voice of our spirit. However, the Lord is keen to teach us in this area, for it is through our fasting that others will be set free to know Him as we do. Much of our Christian labour is impotent due to a lack of fasting. We must not be deceived, prayer intensified with fasting leads to breakthrough in the spirit realm that would not have occurred through "regular" prayer (see Daniel 10).

Too many believers in the West have become cynical and unbelieving. They say that there is only apostasy or apathy here. They have been defeated by the principalities of darkness. Yet they have not seen that victory was always so close to them. All they needed to do was to intensify their warfare by fasting and praying together. In it tragic that so many have fallen when it could have been their greatest hour, if only they had learned to pay a higher price in spiritual things.

The future of England lies in the hands of those who understand these principles. The yoke of bondage is destroyed by fasting. Is not this the fast that I have chosen? to loose the bands of wickedness, to undo the heavy burdens, and to let the oppressed go free, and that ye break every yoke? (Isa 58:6)).

Without fasting our labour will produce a little fruit. Let us therefore consider some issues regarding fasting:

1. Fasting leads to intimacy with God

When we think of Christ fasting we tend to think of Him spending the 40 days struggling the whole time to keep His mind off food, weak for the lack of nourishment, afflicted constantly by the devil. Interestingly the Scripture states that at the end of the forty days Satan came to Him, not during. So what was He really doing during this period? He was spending real quality and quantity time with His Father and His glorious presence.

It wasn't all pain and suffering. As the voice of the flesh is silenced in fasting and our hearts become more sensitive to the Spirit, our passion for God increases. This can lead to glorious times of fellowship with the Father. These are mountain top experiences that bond our hearts closely with His. In this place there is little to interfere with communion and communication with God. I am not saying that the desire to eat disappears. Absolutely not! We are made of flesh and blood and have stomachs that demand sustenance. But the desire to be with the Father supersedes this to the extent that you hardly want to leave the mountaintop.

The Apostle Paul had an intimate relationship with the Lord. He bore much fruit because he was plugged into the vine. He planted churches all around Asia Minor. He wrote much of the New Testament. To him was given the deep revelation of the substitutionary work of Christ on the cross. The Word of God dwelt in him richly so that he became a prophetic voice for his generation and the generations to come. You can't be a mouthpiece for God until you have the heart of God.

It is interestingly to note Paul's personal life of prayer. Remember he was not one of the twelve. He was the apostle "born out of time". He had met the Lord briefly on the road to Damascus. So where did such revelation come from? His intimacy came through spending time with the Lord in prayer and fasting. 2 Corinthians 11.27 tells us he was in "fastings often". He appointed elders to the fledgling churches after times of fasting (no doubt in similar fashion to Jesus appointing his disciples after nights of prayer). His prayer life was frequent and often intensified by fasting.

Our primary reason for fasting is so that we can grow closer to God and so that we can intensify our prayer lives. Don't let this fast go past without spending wonderful quality (and quantity) time with the Lord. Come and join us in the mornings at prayer or in the evening on White Horse hill were we shall be seeking God.

2. Fasting leads to liberty from the world

When you fast the things of the world begin to dim in your view of them. Their hold over you decreases. And to the contrary the things of heaven become more attractive. Try it and see. Conversations about natural things such as films, sports, shopping, funny incidents lose their level of interest for you. Instead you become hungry for the presence of God. It is His presence that produces a satisfaction in you far great than the contentment that comes from having a full belly!

Too often we get entangled in the things of the world. This means we give them too much importance. We spend at least a third of the day buying, preparing, eating and clearing up food. When we fast we have much more time on our hands. Let us be true soldiers of the cross this month. In times of battle there is not much time to stop and eat. There is job to be done; an enemy to conquer. Spend this extra time you have in prayer and spiritual warfare. Your family will be blessed as a result.

3. Fasting leads to victory over the devil

Once our desires for the things of the world is brought into check then the devil's defeat quickly follows. He uses the things of the world to tempt us to serve him. Now his temptations have nowhere to land in our souls. Jesus defeated the devil because His Father's Kingdom was so real to Him. This is one of the reasons that He was not interested to bow the devil in order to win the kingdoms of the world (Matt 4.8-9). When we fast the same becomes true. We are not interested in this world with its false vanities and praise. This world is crucified to us and we are crucified to the world (Gal 6.14).

Fasting also fills us with resolute faith. Jesus said that the disciples could not caste a demon except by prayer and fasting (Matt 17.21). They had tried to work the wonders of God and failed. They were not in the right place. Their faith was not focused. Fasting does that to you. It gets you focused. It gets your spirit on fire. No longer can the flesh cannot dampen out the spirit's passion.

Let us embrace this time of fasting together. The result will be wonderful. We will develop a wonderful intimacy with God and see a real breakthrough in our personal and church life.

TEACHING AS JESUS TAUGHT

And when the Sabbath had come, He began to teach in the synagogue. And many hearing Him were astonished, saying, "Where did this Man get these things? And what wisdom is this which is given to Him, that such mighty works are performed by His hands!

(Mark 6:2)

Many of us see ourselves as students but few of us as teachers. But just as a son becomes a father when he matures, so too must the disciple become a disciple-maker. The freed man frees men. The healed becomes a healer of others. The receiver becomes a giver. The taught becomes a teacher. That is the process of maturity.

Jesus had learned at the hand of His earthly parents, Joseph and Mary, and His heavenly Father. At the age of twelve we find Him in the midst of the scholars of Jerusalem's temple "both listening to them and asking them questions." (Luke 2.46). He was an attentive student.

Later we find Him now teaching what He had learned. It immediately impacted the people around Him. They had never experienced anything like it. It was not just deep and wise but life-transforming.

If there is one thing that the today's world desperately needs, it is teachers in the mould and spirit of Jesus. This is our call as a church of overcomers. Let us consider some principles here:

1. You can only teach what you have learned.

You cannot give what you have not received. You cannot teach what you haven't learned. According to the book of Proverbs, getting wisdom is the principal or first thing you must do in life. Wisdom separates you from the crowd and makes you prosper in no matter what area of life.

Sadly, we have too many messengers without a message. Or even messengers whose message is incomplete or lacking in clarity. Imagine an army messenger arriving and saying to his superiors "The enemy is coming" but does not know from where or when or in what numbers or with what weapons. His message does little to help the situation.

There are few real short cuts in the life of wisdom. What goes in comes out, nothing more and nothing less. Ultimately, only what you learn in the secret place is revealed in the public place. Believers want to have a voice in society but don't want to pay the price of first learning wisdom - and not any kind of wisdom, but the wisdom of God. That is what the world needs whether they know it now or not.

Friends, we go to school to train our brains in the things of this world, but few of us see the importance of training in the things of God. In church circles we pride ourselves in thinking we know all things through reading a few books and listening to Sunday sermons. In reality we are scratching the surface of wisdom and therefore we have a superficial impact on society.

Make your decision today to become a real student of the Word like Jesus was. Book into the next module of the Spiritual Maturity Course now!

2. Wisdom comes to those who have the right attitude of heart.

Have you noticed that two people can read the same scripture and one will be able to draw rich revelation from it, like a seam of gold, and the other dull pickings from the surface. Two people look at the skies and one of them can see all sorts of messages from God in the heavens above that teach him of God's will and ways. But the other just sees the clouds and the sun. The first person sees the sun as a picture of Christ and His faithfulness, His light, His warm, His life. He sees the clouds as a sign of God's protection, His ability to bring water to the thirsty.

What is the difference? One has the right attitude of heart. He wants to learn from God to be pleasing to God. The other wants to learn in order to impress others or gain an accolade. God hides Himself from this latter one. He may know the Word of God but he does not know the God of the Word.

3. If you are faithful with little the Lord will give you much

Have you ever wondered why most of the New Testament was written by a man who was not part of the 12 disciples? Rather, the deep truths of the New Covenant were given to Paul, formerly called Saul of Tarsus, after his conversion on the road to Damascus. Why to him? Yes, indeed, he undoubtedly had a brilliant mind and had been trained in Jewish law by one of the most famous rabbis of his day. But the Lord looks for the right kind of heart more than the right kind of head. So what did he find in Paul's that attracted Him?

Consider this: Paul was faithful to share the revelation that he had with others. "Immediately he preached the Christ in the synagogues, that He is the Son of God". Acts 9.20). Paul preached immediately after his conversion. He did not hold back the revelation that he had. Later in his ministry life he said: "I kept back nothing that was helpful, but proclaimed it to you, and taught you publicly and from house to house." (Acts 20:20). Paul was always faithful with the revelation that God gave him. He shared it immediately with those whom he thought could benefit. He always shared everything he had learned. He gave away his best pearls! For this reason God kept giving him more.

When you share with others what you have learned, then the Lord will give you more revelation. Why would He give such to you if you keep it? When you become a channel then He blesses you.

This is one reason why we are a church of cell groups. The cell leaders teach what they have learned. Then the members, once they have been taught, become leaders of groups and thereby teachers. Each one of us is called to this and through this each one of us grows in wisdom and maturity.

4. The more you are under authority the more authority you have.

One of the things that impacted Jesus's hearers was the authority with which He spoke. "And they were astonished at His teaching, for He taught them as one having authority, and not as the scribes." (Mark 1.22). He spoke with conviction. He knew heaven backed His words.

Where does authority come from? Why were there so many then who taught (and now who teach) but lack authority? Authority comes to a person who is under authority. Jesus marveled at the faith of a Roman centurion who had said to Him, "For I also am a man under authority, having soldiers under me. And I say to this one, 'Go,' and he goes; and to another, 'Come,' and he comes; and to my servant, 'Do this,' and he does it." (Matt 8:9).

Because Jesus was under the direct authority of His Father (and, interestingly, submitted to the prophet of his day, John the Baptist, and his own parents, even though He would have known more than all these people). He had authority. Jesus had been authorized by Heaven, hence His boldness. When you are under God's authority and under the authority of cell leaders and pastors that God puts into our lives, then you will find you will begin to teach with authority.

Please then, teach, teach, teach all that you have learned.

Resting as Jesus rested

"Now it happened, on a certain day, that He got into a boat with His disciples. And He said to them, "Let us cross over to the other side of the lake." And they launched out. But as they sailed He fell asleep."
(Luke 8:22-23)

It is wonderfully comforting to think that Jesus, like us, tired from a days work, could fall asleep in the boat as it slipped across Lake Genessaret to the soft sound of gentle waves breaking on the bow. Just as Mary and Joseph must have marveled that the divine Child had been placed in their care, so now the disciples, no doubt glancing across at their sleeping master, must have felt the awesome privilege of serving and caring for the son of God. He had given them clear instructions, delegated the task to them, and now rested, as you do, when you are confident that people are able to perform it. What could possibly go wrong? That is for another study! Today I would like to focus on the need for us to sleep as Christ slept.

As you read through the gospels it becomes apparent that Christ was always wonderfully rested wherever He went, no matter the pressure and demand on his life. We don't see the signs of tiredness in His life such as sudden irritation and outbursts of harsh words. Jesus always ministered from a place of rest. Stress and the daily pressure is something that we all have to deal with. Hence we must learn to copy Him if we are to retain our health and stay strong through the course of our earthly life. The Lord wants us to be a "rested" people in spirit, soul and body.

1. The rest of God for our spirits

Rest for your spirit comes on the day you are born again. Some people lose this rest because of a misunderstanding of the state of their salvation. They fear they might lose their salvation and so remain in a state of restless anxiety as to whether they are saved or not.

Recently I was travelling with a friend (John Lewis) to Holland. We arrived early at the port to catch the ferry, which turned out to be late. As we had had a 4 am start we decided to sleep whilst we waited in the car. I slept deeply for an hour or more but John slept in fits and starts. Why? He was worried that the ferry would arrive and depart again when he was asleep. He couldn't rest because of the fear of missing the boat. This is understandable.

Too many Christians fear they will miss the boat of salvation! The Scriptures say that we enter rest when we enter Christ. "For we who have believed do enter that rest" (Heb 4.3). We are saved eternally and our future is secure. We cannot lose our salvation. Heaven is our home, God is our Father, His Spirit is the seal that we belong to Him. "Now He who establishes us with you in Christ and has anointed us is God, who also has sealed us and given us the Spirit in our hearts as a guarantee" (2 Cor 1.21-22). Nothing in life or death can separate you from the love of God (Rom 8.38). Relax! Have rest in your spirit.

2. The rest of God for our souls

Rest for our souls comes differently. Romans 8.6 teaches, "To be carnally minded is death but to spiritually minded is life and peace". Rest for your mind and emotions come when our life is in line with the spirit. When it is incongruent you will lose your peace. We have peace when our hearts don't condemn us (1 John 3.21). Are you at peace in your soul or full of anxiety? As soon as you go against the will of the Lord you will lose your peace. This is a way that the Lord steers us away from evil. When you are in the centre of God's will and your mind is fixed on Him you will experience peace in your soul. "You will keep him in perfect peace whose mind is stayed on You, because he trusts in You." (Isa 26.3).

The secret to experiencing the rest of God is to do all that He puts in your heart: nothing more, nothing less and nothing else. Do His daily will and be satisfied. Some people have a messiah complex and feel that they must try and fix everybody's problems. But Jesus did not attempt to do this. Whilst He loved the entire world, He ministered to a limited group of Israelites. He said, "I was not sent except to the lost sheep of the house of Israel." (Matt 15.24). He worked within the limits that His Father had set Him. He ministered to those that God had given Him. He did not try to do too much. Jesus ministered to the multitudes but invested in and cared personally for twelve disciples. It was not possible to do more than this in a day's work. What about you? Do you spread yourself too thinly? Whilst you can minister to all, invest your best into those God gives you to disciple.

3. The rest of God for our bodies

Jesus was an early riser and we read often stayed up beyond sunset healing the masses (Mark 1.32). God wants us to be rested but not lazy. Proverbs 26.14 says, "As a door turns on its hinges, so does the lazy man on his bed". Likewise in Proverbs 6.6, "Go to the ant you sluggard! Consider her ways and be wise". This is no place for idleness in the Kingdom of God (see the parable of the talents).

When you have rest in your spirit and soul, your body will be able to function at higher levels of energy. Congruency produces strength. However, Jesus was also aware of physical limitations. It is comforting to find Him calling His disciples aside to go to rest on a mountain after a hard days work and to see Him sleeping in Peter and Andrew's boat.

Jesus could rest His body because He knew the Father was constantly watching over Him. He is the God who does not "slumber or sleep" (Ps 121.4). Again, He understood the body's physical limitations and submitted Himself to such laws. Some think they are above them and then are surprised when their health fails. Think of your body as a highly sophisticated machine that needs care and attention. Your body needs cleanliness, good food and rest in order to function correctly. It is the temple of the Holy Spirit, so look after it well.

Jesus could rest physically because He could delegate to his disciples. They were beginning to understand His heart and mind. They were obedient to do what He had asked them to do even though they lacked faith when the storm came against them. We too can rest when we raise up people around us who have the same heart and mind. People who love us and care for us, so that, if we are asleep, they will 'carry the ball' or resolve any problems that come up. Sadly, too many human beings do life on their own. They have never raised up disciples or a team of people around them that love and respect them. Hence they have to do everything themselves all of the time. No wonder so many have stressed out or numbed out minds! By investing into those people whom God puts in your life, you will find they become "friends who stick closer than brothers". Life becomes easier; life becomes… more rested.

You will never minister well for God if you are stressed out and tired. The body is the vessel through which God ministers. He is the wind but you are the sail. If the sail is not set correctly the boat won't move forward as it should. A rested body will increase the clarity of your mind, your strength for a day's work, and your ability to conquer the daily challenges of life and the big giants that periodically come your way.

In this way we discover a divine paradox - busy people can be the most rested people on earth.

Dressing as Jesus dressed

"But when the king came in to see the guests, he saw a man there who did not have on a wedding garment. So he said to him, 'Friend, how did you come in here without a wedding garment?' And he was speechless.
(Matt 22:11-12)

Clothes in Scripture speak of many things. We are to be dressed in garments of praise (Isaiah 61.3), be clothed in humility (1Pet 5.5), and wear the robes of righteousness (Rev 19.8). They feature in the beginning with Adam's attempt at covering himself and the Lord's provision of an animal's hide. They feature at the end with the whole host of heaven dressed in white robes (Rev 19.4).

Clothing is obviously an important issue in Scripture. Whilst it is not our intention to lay down rules and regulations, it is clear that there are principles shown in the life of Christ that should govern our choice of attire.

1. Dress to cover, not expose

As a rabbi of His time Christ would have worn long robes in public. They covered his body and from the neck to the ankles. The only parts of his body exposed to the elements where his face, his arms and hands and his feet. This goes in line with how the high priests from the Old Testament would dress. Moses applied the blood of the sacrificial lamb to their right ear and right toe (Lev 8.23). As these were exposed, so they covered by the blood. Likewise whenever an angel's clothing is described we discover that they wear long, white garments.

As noted Adam's attempt at a covering of fig leaves was not sufficient in the eyes of the Lord. Obviously there is a deeper issue than choice of materials. A sacrificial lamb, rather than a branch of a tree, was needed to atone for (or cover) Adam's sin, for 'life is in the blood' (Lev 17.11). But there is a practical issue here as well. Fig leaves do not cover well; animal hides do.

You may think I labour the point but we must be careful here. Firstly, we live in a sensual generation that is perhaps more publicly naked than at any time in history. Clothes are not used so much to cover the body as to expose the body. For instance there is nothing wrong with ladies wearing trousers (as some religious folk may teach) but there is something wrong when those trousers are so tight that all is revealed.

Holy people are discreet people. They don't try to draw attention to themselves through their clothing. A question you should ask yourself each day is; "Am I conscious of the clothes I am wearing? Or, having put them on, can I forget about them?". If the latter is true then it is probable that you are appropriately dressed – neither too dressed up or too dressed down.

We read also that the demon-possessed man in Gardara was later found "clothed and in his right mind", having been set free. Satanic influence had stripped him of clothes, Jesus' influence made him cover himself.

Secondly, there is a principle in Scripture that you should reveal yourselves physically, emotionally and spiritually according to the level of intimacy with the person or people about you. In this way we should be fully clothed in public, but more casual among friends, and the least robed among our own families. The only one you should be completely naked with is your spouse. This principle applies to your inner life as well. Don't expose yourself to strangers. Only reveal your aspirations or anxieties to those with whom you have a level of intimacy. If you are too open with those who don't love you, they will expose you. Ultimately the only person we can be (and are) fully naked before is the Lord.

2. Dress according to the occasion

Some of Christ's disciples were fisherman. To do this hard work they would strip off their outer garments. John 21. 7 says, "Now when Simon Peter heard that it was the Lord, he put on his outer garment (for he had removed it), and plunged into the sea." Wardrobes were smaller in those days but, even so, imagine Peter fishing in his Sunday best! It would not be appropriate.

In like manner, there are appropriate clothes for each occasion. If you are playing sport, you need not (and best not) wear your school uniform! Shorts and t-shirt are fine. There is an appropriate moment to take off outer garments. Don't overdress at times like these - it is religiosity. But if you are going to a wedding don't under-dress. This is not only embarrassing but also disrespectful. You should dress as a way that honours the people you are with. Hence, if the occasion is important or you hold the people in high regard, it is appropriate to dress in a manner that honours them.

In the parable of the wedding feast the underdressed guest is cast out. This does not imply that he loses his salvation but rather he loses his reward in the Kingdom. There are those who are dressed in the clothes of grace by which they are saved, but not the clothes of righteous acts for which they are rewarded. They are inappropriately dressed for the wedding feast, which is the time of reward for the believer.

3. Dress nicely

Due to a Catholic hangover into the reformed church, we tend to see Jesus dressed in shabby clothes, fit for little better than a pauper. This ties in with their doctrine that spirituality is akin to poverty. Hence, in their opinion, for Jesus to be the most spiritual He must have the least of all. This line of thinking states also that Jesus had no home using for reference His saying that "the son of Man has nowhere to lay His head" (Matt 8.20).

The problem with this doctrine is that it does not line up with Scripture and has been taken out of context. Jesus did have a home. When the disciples asked Him where He lived, He replied, "Come and see" (John 1.39). Jesus had "nowhere to lay His head" because He could not rest in this world until He had redeemed it from sin. Only now is He seated (at the right hand of God) because His job is done.

In like manner Jesus' clothes weren't bought from the charity shop equivalent of the day. How do we know? By the simple fact that Roman soldiers, on wages paid by the emperor that far superseded the locals' (think US soldiers in Afghanistan), actually gambled over who would keep Jesus' robe after his crucifixion. This robe must have been of some value; it is not often that people are interested in hanging on to a dead man's clothes, no matter how refined.

In short, Jesus wore nice clothes - not in a way to flaunt or flatter Himself. There was no 'dress to impress' in His manner but rather just good sense. Sadly, today people dress so casually with no sense of what is appropriate, what is respectful, what is pleasant. If the outer world of clothes reveals the inner world of the heart, then much help is needed. You should dress nicely and not be ashamed to do so. And don't do what so many do when a compliment is paid - respond by letting them know that you bought it in a sale at Primark! Just say, “Thank you, I am wearing it to honour you!”

D A Y 7

Eating as Jesus Ate

Then, as soon as they had come to land, they saw a fire of coals there, and fish laid on it, and bread. Jesus said to them, "Bring some of the fish which you have just caught."
(John 21:9-11)

The issue of eating is of more importance today than perhaps ever in history. Our generation is able to find foods from all over the world in the supermarket at the end of the street. In addition, we can prepare them in a flash or eat them ready-made. Processed foods and an increase in food consumption have made modern man bigger and, tragically, unhealthier than his predecessors. Just fifty years ago the common diseases that plagued mankind were contagious external ones such as tuberculosis, but today most diseases come from within, such as cancer and heart disease, many of which are often caused by substance intake.

Yet good food and eating well are one of the great pleasures of life. A holiday is hardly a holiday unless you eat well. Imagine a birthday party without a cake! Food is not just a source of sustenance but also a source of satisfaction and a cause for communion, all of which are important in the Lord's eyes.

So how should we be governed in this area? Once again we are not interested to lay down rules here. The Jewish law is filled with thousands of such regulations - enough to make the mind boggle and the stomach to lose its appetite! We live under the New Covenant where we are permitted to eat all things except things that has been offered to foreign idols or that have been strangled and contain the blood (Acts 15:19).

We are not going to dwell long on what Jesus ate but rather the principles that govern eating. We know He would have eaten a kosher diet, meaning that He was forbidden to eat such things as shellfish and pork, and also that his diet would have been based upon what the local Galilean land produced – hence the main dishes at the time were fish and lamb; the main carbohydrate was bread; and the main vegetables and fruits included olives, grapes, pomegranates among others. Here in England we have many other fruits and vegetables more suited to our climate – courgettes, parsnips and potatoes to name a few. Hence a direct comparison is not helpful or needed. As previously said, let us go beyond the food itself and consider some principles that govern eating.

1. Hunger is a sign of health

Sick people don't like to eat; weak people likewise. At times it is necessary to force feed them or to hover over a reluctant child with a spoonful of food in your hand. The truth is that hunger is a good thing, a sign of health. He who hungers has spent energy and is now craving more sustenance. The cycle of life is in full motion. The principle is spiritual as well. Show me a person who is hungry for the Word of God and I will show you a person who is spiritually healthy. Such a person feasts on the Word of the Lord because they have been spending spiritual energy in the work of the Lord.

Considering this principle it is nice to know that Jesus would have had a healthy appetite. How can we know this? Because He was healthy. In fact Jesus is Health personified.

Some times my children complain and say; "Dad, I'm hungry!" I reply, "That's a great thing. Imagine what it would be like to never hunger?" You see, if you never hunger then you would never be satisfied. Hunger is the prerequisite for satisfaction. Healthy life is a cycle between the two. Jesus said; "Blessed are they that hunger and thirst for righteous for they shall be filled. (Matt 5:6)"

A principle can be found here. Even though you might live and work near a fridge, don't eat all the time. Wait for you hunger to grow. Enjoy that time of increasing desire and expectation. Don't ruin your appetite by having tip-bits between meals - the greater the hunger, the greater the satisfaction. Wait, and then sit down and feast and enjoy. You will eat more healthily and enjoy your food more!

2. You are what you eat

Just as your soul's well-being is determined by what it feasts upon (feed your mind with junk TV and you will live a junky life!) so your body's well-being is determined by what it eats. On a natural level, some of the foods that the Levital Law prohibits are particularly unhealthy. Shellfish for instance is very high in arachidonic acid and saturated fat which predisposes us to disease. Once again should we therefore only eat kosher food? Not according to Scripture; "What God has cleansed do not call unclean"(Acts 11.9). All foods are now clean in the eyes of the Lord and you are free to eat what you like. However, before you live on bacon and chocolate cake for the rest of your life, remember there are deeper principles at stake, the deepest one being the principle of life. If something is negatively affecting your life, then don't do it. In this case, eat such things in moderation as your health is of more importance than your stomach. Too many people of God have not finished their course on earth and gone to early graves because of negligence in this area. When the appetite for food goes unchecked then the dominating force of gluttony slowly destroys the person.

3. Eating together produces intimacy

In the above account in the Gospel of John we find one of the most pleasant scenes in Scripture. Jesus appears to His disciples, after His resurrection, and cooks a breakfast of fish and toast for them on a coal fire on the beach in Galilee. How they must have smiled and hugged and eaten their food with gladness! Some weeks later, after the day of Pentecost, they experienced a similar type of communion over food in the company of the Holy Spirit. "They ate their food with gladness and simplicity of heart." (Acts 2:46)

The Bible links the communion of the saints, or the fellowship of the believers, with "love feasts" (Jude 1.12). Have you noticed that you increase the level of your intimacy with others when you have sat down and eaten together at a table? Something mysterious occurs in the process. By "breaking bread together" your friendship gets closer. You may make acquaintances of people in school or at work, but after you have eaten together you bond closer together and become friends. In ancient times covenants or alliances often included the two parties eating together. Likewise today – a wedding ceremony feels incomplete without the meal to accompany it. This is a covenant meal where the two families, whether they know it or not, are agreeing to side together in an alliance. Of course we believers come together at the Lord's Table for the Lord's Supper and we break bread and drink wine to remember His death (1Cor 11:25-26). This act bonds us together as one intimate family and unites us in alliance in which we live for one another and fight together against a common enemy. All other meals are shadows of this glorious supper. Interestingly, at the Last Supper Christ told His disciples; "I will not drink of the vine until the Kingdom of God comes" (Luke 22:18). This Last Supper is simply the entrée for the Marriage Feast of the Lamb when the Kingdom of God comes in its fullness. To participate correctly in the first supper makes you eligible for the second.

4. Never put physical food above spiritual food

Sadly, too many people err in this area to the grievance of the Lord's Spirit. Christ's disciples themselves needed to learn this lesson. In Samaria they went off to buy food and returned to find Jesus ministering to a woman. When they urged Him to eat He replied: "I have food to eat of which you do not know… My food is to do the will of Him who sent Me, and to finish His work. (John 4:32, 34). For the Lord, doing His Father's work was a type of spiritual food that was more important, and produced an inner joy that was more satisfying, than eating physical food.

Whilst physical food is a blessing, it can become a curse for many, when they prioritize it above the call of God. There are those who don't go to church or cell groups because food is more important. There are those who sit in church thinking of Sunday lunch rather than the Sunday sermon! There are those who plan their lives around food rather than around the will of God. Philippians 3.19 says these people's god is their bellies. They are directed by this the whole time and therefore miss out on God's best for their lives. The principle therefore to live by is this: Eat well and enjoy your food, it is a blessing from the Lord, but whenever spiritual food and physical food clash, choose the former. There is a time to feast, but there is also a time to fast. Sunday lunch always tastes better if you have first been to church!

DAY 8

LEADING AS JESUS LED

Then Peter said, "See, we have left all and followed You."
(Luke 18:27)

Even unbelievers have to conclude that Jesus was a great leader. In three short years He built a team of such loyal followers and created such a mass movement in His nation that the message He shared and the way of life He demonstrated went on to affect every nation under the sun. In addition, He did not start with a group of Oxbridge students, or budding entrepreneurs from The Apprentice! Just as King David, centuries before Him, had built up the Kingdom of Israel with the indebted, the distressed and the discontented, Jesus started with an uneducated, motley crew of fisherman and tax-collectors. Yet, such was His influence that these become the foundational pillars of a trans-cultural, trans-national phenomenon. These men carried such force of character and word that ideologies crumbled before them. If leadership is influence, then Jesus was the most influential leader of all time. If leadership is based on the number of followers, then again, Jesus is the greatest leader of all time.

In our day of life-coaching and self-help books, much has

been made of the need for great leadership. We are told that organisations will rise or fall depending upon the strength of their leadership. We find books written by top C.E.O.s or leading political lights or New Age gurus which urge people to practice certain principles (most of which have been taken from the Bible and put into 'modern-speak'). And yet much of this advice remains superficial. It may help you to be rich but not to be wealthy; it may help you to better your earthly career but not your heavenly one; it may teach you social skills but not deep connection with God and with people; it may equip you to build a big organization but not a living organism. We should not be surprised. If you take out the person of the Bible from the principles of the Bible, then you strip it of its life.

Leadership is exemplified in Christ. He is, after all, not just a Lord, but the Lord of Lords. And yet, incredibly, He becomes so by not "lording" over people. Oh, paradox sublime! That we may grasp it...

In short, Jesus was a leader like none other. It is impossible to separate His person from His principles. Let us consider some differences in Jesus' leadership compared to that of the world:

1. Jesus was focused on heavenly, not earthly, reward

It seems that at every point in which He was tempted, Jesus never compromised His principles for the praise or the prizes of this world. At the beginning of His ministry, when Satan offered Him the Kingdoms of the world, Christ overcame the temptation through the knowledge of the reward laid up for Him in His Father's perfect and pure heavenly Kingdom. When the crowds began to follow Him and the people tried to make Him king, He resisted such promotion or adulation. "When Jesus perceived that they were about to come and take Him by force to make Him king, He departed again to the mountain by Himself alone." (John

6:15). Like His cousin John the Baptist, He did not 'sugar-coat' His words in order to please the adoring crowds. John called the religious leaders a "brood of vipers" and confronted the political leader, Herod, for his immoral ways (Matt 3:7; John 14:4). Jesus, in like spirit, told the Pharisees that there were "of their father the devil" and called Herod a "fox" (John 8:44; Luke 13:32).

When you are not after the praise of people, you are able to speak with the liberty and authority of heaven. The truth becomes the key issue. Jesus was resolute when many followers decide to leave because they found His teaching too hard to receive (John 6:66). Why? Because His desire was to hear the Father say to Him, "Well done my good and faithful servant, you were faithful over a few things, I will make you ruler over many things. Enter into the joy of your lord.'(Matt 25:21). He Himself had taught that if you receive the praise of men then you will not receive the praise of God (Matt 6:2). But if you forsake the desire of this world, great is your reward in heaven

Now, with all respect to leaders in business or politics, their goal and motivation may be very different. A business leader may make a decision based on what makes the most money, rather than on what is the right thing to do. Likewise politicians may make decisions that please the electorate rather than choosing what is right to do, because they fear not being elected again.

2. Jesus served His followers, they did not serve Him

You never read about Jesus imploring His disciples to help Him build His ministry or fulfill His earthly purpose. Much less do we find Him with a proverbial begging bowl in His hands crying out, "Unless you give, then we are going under!"

Jesus provided for His disciples as a father provides for his sons. There was food to eat when they were hungry (Mark 6:44); there was fish for their nets when they had exhausted their own efforts (John 21:6); there was even money for the taxman when they were short of it (Matt 17:27). He did not depend on them, rather they depended upon Him.

No parent wants to become dependent upon their children for support, especially when they are in their prime and should be providing for the family. There is a shame that people feel if they depend upon those who should depend on them.

Sadly, many leaders today seem to depend on others to keep themselves propped up. They do not see their role as a fatherly one in which they give their best to the children: rather, they keep the best for themselves and put around them people whom they feel can help. They 'milk' their followers and discard them once their use is over.

Christ-like leadership thinks differently. Christ did not come to be served but to serve (Matt 20:28). He washed the feet of His disciples, not the other way around. The reason why we are nice to the affluent and indifferent to the needy when they come into our churches is because we want something that the rich have. We do not see them as people to be served but as people who should serve us.

Oh, tragedy! How far we have fallen into the world's ways! Jesus did not want any of the rich young ruler's money. Rather He told him to give it away (Matt 19:21). In like manner, Elisha wanted no payment for healing Naaman the Syrian (2 Kings 5:16).

No wonder the church has lost its cutting edge in the Western world... we have been too easily bought out.

3. Jesus never asked anyone to do what He hadn't done

"If anyone desires to come after Me, let him deny himself, and take up his cross, and follow Me." (Matt 16.24). Jesus was able to ask people to deny themselves and take up their cross, because He had done it. In fact no man has ever carried a cross as heavy as our Lord's or denied Himself to such extremes. Even His death is supreme, compared to the martyrdom of the greatest saints. When captured or attacked they had no way out; but Christ could have called angels to come and rescue Him (Matt 26:53) yet He resisted.

Leaders lose their influence when they delegate tasks that they are not willing to do themselves or challenge people to a level of sacrifice that they are not willing to pay themselves. Followers might obey but they do so reluctantly. When a leader is willing to lower himself to our station, even though he may be far more able, as Christ Himself was, then our hearts are touched to such a degree that we willingly desire to do the same for others. We have experienced a true compassion and a deep sympathy that makes us want to show the same towards others.

David raised up an army of mighty men who were willing to risk their lives for him, because he had risked his life for them on many occasions, starting with the defeat of Goliath. Paul raised up dedicated disciples and church leaders in cities all around the Mediterranean because they had seen that no cost was to great for him to pay for their well-being. If these men of old had such influence over entire nations, surely that can happen again if today's leaders are equally Christ-like. Come, let's walk together and see…

Drinking as Jesus drank

And when they ran out of wine, the mother of Jesus said to Him, "They have no wine." Jesus said to her, "Woman, what does your concern have to do with Me? My hour has not yet come." His mother said to the servants, "Whatever He says to you, do it."
(John 2:3-5)

If gluttony is the demon of food excess, then drunkenness is the demon of drink excess. No doubt extremes are to be avoided. But is there any middle ground on this issue of drinking for the believer? Or are we to do as many have done, that is, to make abstention a doctrine? Did Jesus drink? If so, when, what and in what manner? If He is our model and Paul our model imitator, then let us look to them so that we might navigate this difficult path.

1. Spiritual wine is superior

The first thing to note from Scripture is that spiritual drink is always superior to physical drink. What physical drink is to our bodies, spiritual drink is to our spirits. Life comes in through our spirits, and this spiritual life is as far superior as the heavens are above the earth.

At the marriage feast in Cana the extraordinary incident occurs that every Sunday school boy knows about, that of Jesus turning water into wine. For me, the change of material matter is not the most remarkable thing in the story. But let us start with a couple of observations. Firstly, when Jesus is informed of the lack of wine and asked by His mother to help, He does not react with hostility, as perhaps many believers today would do. He does not refuse to have anything to do with the alcohol and be involved in such sin. Rather, He seems remarkably peaceable. We might deduce that in His mind, wine was a substance that could be used for good or for evil, depending on the user. Jesus' main concern was to cover the shame of the host and meet the need of the guests. This is done and new wine is produced in abundance and with greater quality, for such is the Kingdom of God.

But more interesting to me is the Lord's response to His mother; "Woman, what does your concern have to do with Me? My hour has not yet come." (John 2:4). At first glance this seems like a rather firm 'put down' to His dear mother. That is until you zoom out and see the bigger picture. Christ was of a heavenly mindset and on a heavenly mission. At times people asked Him questions on a natural plane and He answered them on a spiritual plane. Christ's purpose on earth was not so much to turn physical water into wine but to turn the common into the exotic, 'lumps of coal into nuggets of gold', sons of men into sons of God. His role was to release heavenly wine on earth. His "hour" for this had "not yet come". For that could only be achieved through His death and resurrection and then the sending of the Spirit once He had been glorified, not before (see John 7.39). Then the true heavenly wine would be released to earth.

This prophetic purpose, first uttered by the prophet Joel,

was fulfilled at Pentecost and noted by Peter, who answered the people's criticism that the disciples were drunk with wine by saying; "These men are not drunk as you suppose" (Acts 2:13-15). In other words, they had been drinking a different type of wine. Jesus Himself spoke of this heavenly substance: "But new wine must be put into new wineskins, and both are preserved" (Luke 5:38).

It is this 'new wine' experience that human beings both need and ultimately are looking for. Old wine can't satisfy but new wine can. It is by drinking from heavenly fonts that we thirst no more (John 4:14). Hence Paul says; "And do not be drunk with wine, in which is dissipation; but be filled with the Spirit" (Eph. 5:18).

Here's my point; always be passionate about being filled with the Spirit, each and every day. This is the only thing that will satisfy your heart. Don't try to substitute that with the wine of this world. You will be very disappointed and miss out on the best Christ has for you.

2. Earthly drinks must be handled with care

But should we therefore never drink, or is there something good in it? Firstly, the Scripture seems to make a distinction between drink and strong drink. Strong drink is to be handled with extreme care for it causes brawling and bitterness (Prov. 20:1 & Isa. 24:9). Into this category we must put all spirits/liquors, which have high alcohol percentages due to being distilled.

Un-distilled drinks, such as wine, fall into a different category. Despite the fact that Scripture also gives warning to those who do drink them, wine is described as something brought forth by God for our enjoyment: "That he may bring forth food from the earth, And wine that makes glad the heart of man" (Ps. 104:15). Jesus Himself implied that He drank wine. "For John came neither eating nor drinking, and they say, 'He has a demon.' The Son of Man came eating and drinking, and they say, 'Look, a glutton and a winebibber" (Matt 11:18-20). Of course, as noted, wine was present at the feast of Cana and at the Last Supper.

Paul gives clarity to the issue when talking of the appointment of leaders in the church. He says that they must not be "given to wine" (Titus 1:7) and the older women should not be "given to much wine" (Titus 2:3). Here is moderation and self-control. Good sense says that if you do enjoy a glass of wine make sure that your consumption of it does not dilute your dedication to the Lord.

3. The strong must help the weak

Whatever the case, there are times when believers should never consider having a drink. These are when your drinking may cause someone else to stumble. In other words, if that 'someone' is not able to drink with restraint then it is best that he does not drink at all, nor be encouraged to drink by those around him. By drinking at times like this you may cause him to fall into sin, and your lack of care and restraint has been part of the cause. As we should flee from sin at all costs, so we should abhor the thought of someone falling into sin because of us. Paul writes: "It is good neither to eat meat nor drink wine nor do anything by which your brother stumbles or is offended or is made weak" (Rom. 14:21).

"But this may limit my freedom to drink", you complain. "Yes, indeed, it may." But that is precisely the point. You should be willing to sacrifice things for the sake of the ministry of Christ, in order not to bring dishonor to His name and to help others stand perfect for the Lord. If you think that you have self-control in this area (and you should only drink at all if you do have), then you should be able to abstain whenever it is appropriate. Mature people don't just think of their own delights and desires but first and foremost of the well-being of the people around them.

Forgiving as Jesus forgave

Then Peter came to Him and said, "Lord, how often shall my brother sin against me, and I forgive him? Up to seven times?" Jesus said to him, "I do not say to you, up to seven times, but up to seventy times seven.

(Matt 18:21-22)

God's standard for forgiveness is shockingly higher than human standards. Yet He is our standard and He expects the same of us. Jesus said, "Therefore you shall be perfect, just as your Father in heaven is perfect" (Matt. 5:48). His earliest disciples practiced the same level of forgiveness as He did. Just as Christ released forgiveness on the cross of Calvary with the immortal words "Father, forgive them, for they do not know what they do." (Luke 23:34), so too Stephen forgave those who were stoning him to death for his faith. The Scripture says; "Then he knelt down and cried out with a loud voice, "Lord, do not charge them with this sin" (Acts 7:60).

Let us learn today how to be imitators in this fundamental area of forgiveness by considering the following points:

1. We must forgive no matter HOW MANY times we are offended

Peter had thought he would impress the Lord by declaring that he would forgive someone up to seven times. This, in his mind, was height of spirituality. Yes, he would be a real disciple and not just forgive once or twice but seven times! But Jesus blows this attempt at godliness out of the water. He corrected him with "seventy times seven". You see, God's ways are higher than man's ways, as the heavens are above the earth. Man's level forgiveness, even at its best, falls way short of God's standard.

C.S. Lewis famously said: "Everyone thinks forgiveness is a good thing, until it is their turn to forgive!" We would do well to remember that forgiveness is not a feeling. To the contrary, it goes against our feelings! I have rarely felt as if I wanted to forgive in the moment of being injured. When we are offended, our natural tendency is towards retribution. We want to hurt the person who hurt us! Even if we don't say it out aloud to the person, a little voice within says, "I'm going to make you pay!" In this moment Sin is crouched at the door of our hearts. We must act quickly and shut it out through the act of forgiveness.

So, if forgiveness is not a feeling, what then is it? It is a decision. We decide to forgive. The decision to forgive is to be made each and every time an offence is received. Now, most people will agree with this; but let us go a little further. What if the person offending you does it again and again and again? We think that, surely, there should be a limit to the amount of forgiveness we give. Within us we carry a little device that measures the depth and the frequency of offence. When a certain, arbitrary level is passed then we feel justified if we revenge ourselves by fighting back, criticizing, wishing ill on the person and even planning ways to make them suffer.

But hold on! Let us listen to Christ once again. He is our model and we are to be His imitators. We are to forgive, not just once or twice but seven times seventy times or however many times is necessary. Think differently from now on: determine to be a forgiver - all the time and without exception. Retribution is not in the Christian's remit or responsibility. After all "vengeance" belongs to the Lord, not to us (Rom. 12:19).

2. We must forgive no matter HOW GRAVE the offence

Now, we cannot compare any trespass against us with the injustice that Jesus suffered at His trial and crucifixion. It would pale in comparison. The truth of the matter is that our sins against God are always much greater than the sins that others have committed against us.

"Can this be true?" you ask. "I know I am not perfect, but my trespasses are small compared to the way other people have trespassed against me!" We forget that what we consider small sins may be great crimes in Heaven's eyes. Sin is both rejection of God's Counsel and rebellion against His Authority. It is both high treason against the King of Righteousness and siding with His arch-rival, Satan, whether you were aware of it or not. You may have only told a little "pork pie", but in reality, you have sided with the father of lies and through lying, destroyed honesty and trust – the very fabric of family life and stable society as a whole. The Lord has forgiven you of all this. In comparison, forgiving others now is not so demanding. Better get on and do it quickly or....

3. We must forgive in order TO PREVENT being contaminated by the offence

Let me explain. Read the following warning of the Lord. Things are rarely more seriously emphasized than this: 'You wicked servant!

I forgave you all that debt because you begged me. Should you not also have had compassion on your fellow servant, just as I had pity on you?' And his master was angry, and delivered him to the torturers until he should pay all that was due to him. "So My heavenly Father also will do to you if each of you, from his heart, does not forgive his brother his trespasses." (Matt 18:32-35)

Stern words which we would be wise to remember! We had better deal with our moodiness and bad attitudes quickly. The torture He speaks of starts today, let alone in the age to come. If you do not forgive the wrongdoing that you have suffered, that very wrong will begin to eat you up on the inside in the form of bitterness, anger and hate. The only way to stop the poison of offence from remaining in you, once you have been offended, is to open your heart in forgiveness. Through this, the healing river of God both cleanses you and also washes over the people who caused the offence. Remember, it is through the "stripes" (wounds of offense) of Jesus that we are healed (Isa. 53:5). In other words, the very fact that He released forgiveness to His crucifiers whilst He was on the cross, kept Him uncontaminated and opened up a channel of healing to all who look to Him.

Does healing power gush from your wounds? Or do you still carry bitterness and resentment towards others? Become a healer not a hurter of others. Forgive, and you will experience the blessing of God and be a blessing wherever you go.

4. We must forgive in the MANNER that the Lord deals with the offence

For the Lord, to forgive is to forget. Not in the sense of a fault in mental recall but rather, in the sense of choosing not to remember. "Their sins and their lawless deeds I will remember no more" (Heb. 10:17). In other words, to forgive and not forget is incomplete forgiveness.

Many couples suffer because the spouses keep in mind a list of offences from the past. They build their case against their "accused" based on this evidence. In fact, their minds are already biased towards interpreting present-day actions in the light of this past experience. Not so with the Lord! Every day is a new day with Him; just as the sun rises and the dew is fresh on the ground, so too He views us anew after every dark night of failure.

Throw away your lists my friends, and start again! Forget the past and focus on the future! Don't even discuss it… it will only make things worse. Remember, as soon as you start accusing, you are in the employ of "the Accuser of our souls" (Rev 12:10). Start afresh today with a clean slate… and tomorrow too, if that is necessary…and the day after, too… until seven times seventy (or ad infinitum). Only then are you practicing Jesus' type of forgiveness. If we are honest, each one of us needs the dew of forgiveness each morning, so let us be quick to extend it to others.

5. We must forgive to UNBLOCK the heavens

Jesus prayers were always answered. What about ours? Sometimes they may not be because we "ask amiss", out of a desire to satisfy our carnal pleasures (James 4:3). But other times because our prayers have been hindered due to the lack of forgiveness in our hearts. Jesus taught; "First be reconciled to your brother, and then come and offer your gift." (Matt 5.24). Peter later said; "Husbands… giving honor to the wife, as to the weaker vessel, and as being heirs together of the grace of life, that your prayers may not be hindered. (1Pet 3:7)

The principle is clear: if you harbor unforgiveness the heavens will be brass. However, forgive others and the heavens will open to you and God's power and favour can and will come down. Too often we doubt the power of our prayers because they are not answered, but perhaps the blockage is with us and not with heaven? Perhaps, God has been wanting to send revival and heal our land but cannot until His people learn to forgive one another? It is another case of us waiting for God when, all the time, God has been waiting for us"!

D A Y 11

Believing like Jesus believed

So Jesus answered and said to them, "Have faith in God. For assuredly, I say to you, whoever says to this mountain, 'Be removed and be cast into the sea,' and does not doubt in his heart, but believes that those things he says will be done, he will have whatever he says. Therefore I say to you, whatever things you ask when you pray, believe that you receive them, and you will have them.

(Mark 11:22-24)

Sometimes when we consider the life of Christ we fall into the trap of recognizing Him as the Son of God but not as the Son of Man. We see Him thinking such sublime thoughts and doing such supernatural deeds because of His heavenly origins. We feel that miracles and knowing the will of God was "easy" for Him because of this. We like to think that He had a special hotline to God that He could call on anytime. But, we tell ourselves; in comparison we are in inferior person and in a lower position - we aren't equipped with special powers (quite in the same way); and God doesn't speak to us in the same clarity. Deep down within there is a part of us that excuses our own lack of faith on these grounds. Yet what we forget is that Jesus actually lived performed miracles as a man of faith rather than as a God of power. The Bible says that He emptied Himself.... and became a man just as we are (Phil 2:7-8).

Our theology must be clear in this aspect. Christ was the second Adam and came to win back what the first Adam had lost... as a man. Had He resorted to his divinity, the game, so to speak, would have been lost, for He would have broken the rules. In the same way it would be unfair for Superman to compete in the boxing ring but perfectly just if Clark Kent put on the gloves! Christ lived as a man, was tempted as a man, prayed as a man, and worked miracles as a man.

What we are saying is that Christ moved mountains because of his faith alone. Obviously such faith released the anointing of the Spirit that was upon Him. But is was His faith, living and active, that caused the dead to raise and the blind to see and sea to calm. It was not a simple case of "sprinkling angel dust that He had picked up from heaven."

When we stop to consider this fully, we realize that He was no different than us in this aspect. We too are sons of Men. We too have received an anointing from the Holy One. The only thing that is missing is the same level of faith in our hearts. This is what differentiates us from Him. It is what differentiates believers too. David had faith, when Saul did not. Therefore David was an overcomer whilst Saul was overcome.

Bible teachers, such as EW Kenyon, have pointed out the better translation for "Have faith in God" (Mark 11:22) is "Have the faith of God", or in other words, "Have the God kind of faith". Now this changes everything. Now we can focus on the issue. How are we to have the faith that He had? How can we believe as He believed?

Here are some principles that show you the difference

between the type of faith that people have and the type of faith that Jesus had:

1. We must face the facts - Jesus spoke of mountains.

The first precondition for a miracle is having an immovable problem. We all have "mountains" in our lives that block our paths and our progress. Our destinies, like and winding adventure trail, lie on the other side of the mountains. We face them and must decide whether we will conquer them or return back to the plains of mediocrity. Many a person, dominated by their senses, has taken this path of least resistance. But there are some who sense they were born for such challenges.

Jesus spoke of mountains. He did not pretend that they do not exist. His is not a message of mere positive-thinking. The mountains that He is referring to, represent problems that appear enormous, immovable and interminable - those things that you can't change to matter what you try and that have been in your life for too long already and don't look as if they will be leaving soon. They are troubles that are as old as the mountains. They manifest as debt-mountains, sickness-mountains, or relationship-mountains.

Jesus never asks us to fake the facts but to face the facts. These are real issues – big ugly giants that could destroy our lives.

2. We must see the facts by faith - Jesus spoke of the sea

Yet Jesus is also asking us to come up to a higher level. As those of you who have flown over the Alps will know, even mountains look small from the skies. Jesus operated at this level and so must we too. He kept a heavenly perspective. He stood on the mountain of the Lord and viewed the mountains of the men. The difference was great. The Lord's mountain is eternal and consistent, made from the rock of ages and at its heart is solid gold. At closer inspection the mountains that we face are subject to change. There are cracks in its body, for it is a kingdom divided against itself and it cannot stand (Mark 3:24). It is built upon the shifting sands of change that have no depth or foundation.

Like the Iron Curtain or the Communist ideology, things that looked like they are unshakeable, end up crumbling before us. The "impossible" happens. The doctor's report changes, the bank's demand letters dry up, and the chasm between spouses disappears.

Where are these mountains to be cast? Jesus said to the sea. The sea in Scripture speaks of two things: death and forgetfulness. The things that dominated us through fear and towered over us, as Goliath over David, now lie dead at our feet. We wonder how we were so afraid in the first place now. Like a blow up bouncy castle, their size is diminished now the life has been sucked out of them.

We also talk of things being washed away in the sea of forgetfulness. The mother forgets the pain of childbirth for the miracle has happened. During the labour it seemed as if it was an impossible mountain to surmount. But now it is over and lies behind us, below us, and is slowly washed away like a sandcastle in the upcoming tide. The Egyptian army that had oppressed the Israelites with an iron hand for generations were now not just dead in the sea but washed away by it. The physical pain was gone but also the emotional pain was replaced with joy!

3. We must apply faith to the facts - Jesus spoke to the mountains.

Our mountains cast into the sea? Oh joy! "How so?" we ask. Let's look to Jesus; He is the author and finisher of our faith (Heb 12.1-2).

Jesus used spoken words to defeat the devil in the wilderness. In like manner David confronted the giant with words, well before he threw the stone and used the sword. Words come first. Not any kind of word but rather the word of faith – words of command, words of instruction, words of authority.

When Jesus believed He spoke. When Jesus spoke mountains moved. Sometimes they moved immediately – the spirit of infirmity that had bound a woman for eighteen years was bound itself and she was set free (Mark 13:11). Sometimes it was a process – the fig tree that He cursed had its sap cut off and shortly after withered away (Mark 11.20). No matter the length of time, His Word was powerful and the material and spiritual realm responded.

Here we must learn and learn quickly, for our own lives and the lives of those around us depend upon it. We must begin to speak to our mountains. People may accuse you of being drunk with new wine (Acts 2:13), but if you want to have breakthrough in your life you need to lift up your voice and begin proclaim with faith the promises of God. Don't remain silent. Don't sit there and think; "Well Jesus knows my need and He knows my address to visit me!" If blind Batimaeus had thought the same, Jesus would have passed him by and his predicament unchanged (Mark 10:46).

When David stood in the huge shadow of the man-mountain Goliath, he spoke out words of faith; Hence his utterance, "This day the Lord will deliver you into my hands…"(1Sam 17:46).

Remember too that speaking to the mountain is much different than speaking about the mountain. Discussing your problem with others may just increase the size of it. This may bring you sympathy but it won't bring you solution.

Strange though it may sound, but power is released through

the spoken word – whether for good or for evil. Make your words count. There is a miracle in your mouth! Speak with conviction, with your mind fully made up on the issue. Just as parents delight when the child is very sure of want he wants, so too the Lord responds to those who ask with clarity, conviction and confidence.

SHEPHERDING AS JESUS SHEPHERDED

"I am the good shepherd. The good shepherd gives His life for the sheep. But a hireling, he who is not the shepherd, one who does not own the sheep, sees the wolf coming and leaves the sheep and flees; and the wolf catches the sheep and scatters them. The hireling flees because he is a hireling and does not care about the sheep. I am the good shepherd; and I know My sheep, and am known by My own

(John 10:11-14)

Before you turn off and think that this teaching does not apply to you, let me define shepherding or pastoring for you. It is to care for and nourish people. It is to protect and to provide for them, to develop and mature them in a safe environment. Since all of us are called to be ministers (servants of others) then are all called to shepherd. We do this for our families and our cell groups and for those we win for Christ. We even shepherd people in our business organisations.

Once again, here we find that Jesus' way of shepherding is a world apart from much of which is practiced today. It is no coincidence that He calls Himself the "Good Shepherd". The implication is that there were -and are -"bad" ones.

Historically, Israel suffered terribly at the hands of their leaders – those who should have cared for them actually misused them. In Ezekiel chapter 34 we read God's complaint against such: "Woe to the shepherds of Israel who feed themselves! Should not the shepherds feed the flocks? You eat the fat and clothe yourselves with the wool; ....The weak you have not strengthened, nor have you healed those who were sick, nor bound up the broken, nor brought back what was driven away, nor sought what was lost; but with force and cruelty you have ruled them."

In the Gospels we read Jesus' complaint against the "bad shepherds" of His day:

Woe to you, scribes and Pharisees, hypocrites! For you devour widows' houses, and for a pretense make long prayers ... Woe to you, scribes and Pharisees, hypocrites! For you cleanse the outside of the cup and dish, but inside they are full of extortion and self-indulgence. (Matt. 23:14, 25)

Into this context Jesus presents Himself as the "Good Shepherd". We would do well to learn from Him. Rather than pointing your finger at others, let these definitions of a good shepherd shape you:

1. Good shepherds give protection

The main difference between a good shepherd and bad one is the fact that the good shepherd is a giver whereas the bad shepherd is a taker. Jesus noted that there were "hirelings" – those who were paid a wage to look after the sheep but who did not own or genuinely care for the sheep. For them, they were little more than a source of income.

Jesus, however, is the Shepherd who was dedicated to

protecting the flock from the savage attacks of the wolf, Satan. He protected them from storms; He defended them from accusation; He prayed for them from the beginning to the end of His ministry; He interceded for Peter when under serious satanic scrutiny; He warned them incessantly of the devil's wolfish ways. Finally, He gave His life to protect them from Satan's most formidable weapon, Sin itself.

Now, let us consider ourselves. How much of our life is spent in the service of others? Do we consider those around us to be simply a drain on our time, energy and resources? Worse still, do we cross over the proverbial street to avoid them? Is our goal to use the people and resources around us to make our own lives comfortable? For such is the attitude of hirelings. They use people for their own benefit and, if someone is deemed of no use, they are treated with disdain.

Some shepherds have the attitude that they are far too good for the people around them; that their gifting is being wasted in such an environment; that they are never recognized for their true talent. Hence they leave whenever a better opportunity presents itself. Good shepherds don't and can't think like that. They understand that the Lord has entrusted precious people into their hands. They cannot abandon them. They are thrilled that they have any sheep at all to look after, rather than always feeling that they deserve much more. They are faithful with the ones that the Lord gives to them. They dedicate themselves to protecting those ones from the attacks of the enemy.

2.Good shepherds give provisions

A good shepherd furnishes rather than 'fleeces' the flock. His concern is not just to protect the sheep from enemy attack but also that the sheep would grow healthily. He wants to take them to a "Shalom" environment – a place of peace and prosperity. Healthy growth depends upon the grass which they eat. A good shepherd knows that, at times, the best grass is not that which is closest. He may need to lead them up the hills or into distant valleys to find this nourishment.

Good shepherding of the Lord's flock relies on the same principle. Firstly, we shepherd the flock by driving back the enemy in prayer. Ours is a spiritual battle, for the devil goes around like a roaring lion looking for a sheep that he might devour it (1 Pet. 5:8). Hence every shepherd must pray constantly for his sheep. Every cell group leader must constantly ask the Lord to protect His flock.

Secondly, he should be passionate about providing the flock with good food. The best food is not often in the local convenience store. Most of the time you need to drive to a decent supermarket to get it. In like manner, leaders cannot be satisfied with spiritually light sermons for their flocks – this will make the flock anemic, weak and sickly. A good shepherd spreads a banquet of spiritual food before the flock on a weekly basis.

Pastors, leaders, parents and disciple-makers, must take care to not just regurgitate a bible teaching but to study it until it sets their own hearts on fire. Only then can they serve a 'hot dish' before their people. Remember, lukewarm messages are no better than lukewarm dinners – they are fit only for the bin!

3. Good shepherds give affection

Jesus knew His sheep and also was known by them. Both are necessary for affection to truly exist. To know your sheep starts with counting and valuing every one under your care. Jesus counted His sheep – He would know, if he had ninety-nine, that one was lost. Jesus also knew His disciples intimately. He knew their stories, their temperaments, their strengths and their weaknesses. When He got into Peter and Andrew's boat, He got into their world (Luke 5:2). And when He invited His first disciples to His home, they got into His world (Jn 1:39)

Of course He could not have the same level of intimacy with the multitude. He limited Himself to the Twelve but also commissioned the Twelve to do the same with their own disciples. In this way the One Hundred and Twenty were cared for (Acts 1). In like manner, Jethro had advised Moses, centuries before, so that all the people we covered and cared for (Exod. 18:17-23). We today imitate this model by having cell groups. In such an environment everyone enjoy rich friendships and proper pastoral care.

It is one thing to know the flock and another thing to be known by them. Jesus did not stand aloof from the disciples. He did not deem their presence to be beneath Him. He opened His life to them. They could look into His heart and marvel. Strangely, there are some shepherds in the Church who detach themselves from their disciples. They are islands out on their own, untouchables; they act as members of a type of spiritual royal family. Perhaps they do not want people to look too closely into their hearts?

As with a good shepherd, Jesus is known by His sheep. They know His voice, His message, His heart. They can recognize His voice in a crowded room. They can recognize it even when a thousand contradictory doctrines are placed before them. They find comfort and rest in His voice, for they know that He will always lead them to good pastures, where they can lie down and rest.

When shepherds are good, when we shepherd as Jesus shepherded, the soul of the flock is restored – people start thinking correctly about themselves, their emotions come into balance, and they become able to make the right decisions for their lives. When you are looked after by a good shepherd (a faithful imitator of the

Great Shepherd of Israel) you begin to exult in the way David did: "The Lord is my shepherd; I shall not want. He makes me to lie down in green pastures;

He leads me beside the still waters. He restores my soul" (Psalm 23:1-3)

Rejoicing as Jesus Rejoiced

Nevertheless do not rejoice in this, that the spirits are subject to you, but rather rejoice because your names are written in heaven." In that hour Jesus rejoiced in the Spirit and said, "I thank You, Father, Lord of heaven and earth, that You have hidden these things from the wise and prudent and revealed them to babes. Even so, Father, for so it seemed good in Your sight.

(Luke 10:20-21)

For this teaching you need to throw off any high-church mindset you may have about Jesus. He has surprised us already many times in this study of Him. While some people may be comfortable seeing Jesus as a joyful person, fewer can imagine Him really rejoicing or, perchance, laughing. Crying, yes! We can see Him crying for we feel that crying is spiritual. But laughing, no! Such an image does not fit the 'churchy' perception of Him.

Yet to be joyful is a divine attribute. Psalm 2:4 says, "He who sits in the heavens shall laugh". Obviously we are not talking about the kind of laughter that comes as a reaction to coarse humour but rather a deep holy laughter that is an expression of a spirit exulting in the ways of the Lord.

Jesus is a fountain of joy. Talking of Him, the Bible says, "Your God has anointed You with the oil of gladness more than Your companions" (Heb. 1:9). Wherever He went He was good news. Indeed, where the Gospel was preached, great joy came to those cities (Acts 8:8). He is not all solemnity and somberness, as some would have it. They cry out "But Scripture says He was a 'man of sorrows!'" (Isaiah 53:3). Indeed, He was, when He took on the sin of the world. You would be, too, if someone laid a hard wooden cross on your back and led you off to your crucifixion. However, it also says, "for the joy that was set before Him, He endured the cross" (Heb. 12:2). In other words, He was sorrowful that day but joy was on the way.

I dare you to see Jesus again – this time He is smiling from ear to ear – such is His delight in converts streaming into His Kingdom from every corner of the earth and His Father being glorified in all the nations.

Let us consider the purpose, time and reason for joy:

1. The purpose of joy

None of us doubt the strength of Christ's faith, His resolve, His passion and His power. What was the source of such strength? His joy! To be joyless, according to Scripture, is to be powerless for "the joy of the Lord is your strength" (Neh. 8:10). Said differently, the strongest believers are the most joyful ones. That does not mean that we are not serious too. In fact, we are serious about our joy!

The Church in the West continues to struggle with this idea. Our theology has made dry and emotionless believers of us. The Christian life is seen as a struggle to be endured rather than an abundant life to be enjoyed. No wonder we have become so impotent in modern culture! Restore joy to the believer and you restore his strength. A cell group that laughs together is a cell group that advances and grows. A church that has a weekly celebration service in practice, rather than just in name, is a church that conquers and grows.

Have you noticed how children laugh more than adults? It is because they have no guile. This is a godly characteristic. Jesus commends Nathaniel for being like this (John 1:47). We could conclude that guile or deceit stops people from rejoicing. As there is no deceit in Christ, He must be joy itself. No wonder the children liked to be with Him during His earthly ministry (Matt. 19:14).

2. The time for joy

Ecclesiastes 3:1,4 says, "To everything there is a season, a time for every purpose under heaven: ...A time to weep, and a time to laugh".

So there are appropriates times to laugh. People who laugh at the wrong time for the wrong reason need to be corrected. For instance a child who laughs at someone who is disabled must be set straight. It is not right to laugh at the misfortune of another – it is at best silliness and at worst wickedness.

Children actually need to be taught by parents what they should laugh at. They are great imitators. I remember as a child being so attracted by my father's laugh. If he was watching television and laughing, I would go and sit with him just to try to laugh at the things he laughed at. It was infectious. Now, the same thing happens with my children. If they ever watch a funny movie they want me to watch with them, especially the funny bits, because they want to laugh with my laugh.

Our children are very impressionable, which is why we must

learn to laugh at the right things. But what concerns me here is that there are households that rarely hear laughter. Have you lost your laugh? Come and join us at a cell or a celebration meeting. There we can all dive into the river of joy together and "splash around" in the presence of the Lord, for "there is a river whose streams shall make glad the city of God" (P.s 46:4). The Lord has turned our mourning into dancing and replaced the spirit of heaviness with the oil of joy (Isaiah 63:3).

3. The reason for joy

Jesus rejoiced for good reason. He saw Satan falling like lightning, cast out, not just by angels in heaven, but now also by believers on earth. The victory was now complete. The devils' destiny has been decided by heaven and earth, by God and His people. He had come to seduce humankind into accepting him as lord. But his cover has been exposed and Man has risen up and taken the side of God. God did not compel us to throw Satan out. He gave man light to see and power to act should he so desire. Man did. Hallelujah! Jesus' joy is in victory. (The enemy of heaven is to be cast from earth too.)

We too rejoice today with good reason ... we rejoice not because the devil in subject to the Lord's name, but because our names are written in the Lamb's book of Life. Now, if this does not make you happy then nothing can. Have you stopped to consider that you are going to live in eternal bliss in the presence of God and His angels forever? How can that thought not put a smile on your face? "A merry heart makes a cheerful countenance" (Prov.15:13). Really, if this revelation sinks into your spirit, you should be waking up every morning wanting to dance and sing in the knowledge of your eternal future.

We rejoice because we sense the joy of the Lord in our hearts. The Spirit in us expresses what the Lord Jesus is enjoying now. He is sitting at God's right hand in heaven. He has won the victory. The victory song that He sings with the angels is the song in our hearts. Consequently "Joy" is one of the nine Fruit of the Spirit (Gal. 5:22).

In God's presence is fullness of joy (Ps. 16:11). His presence is in you, giving you an inner joy that the world does not have and that the world can't take away. This inner joy comes bubbling out whenever appropriate. At times Jesus turns the fountain of living water into wine – that is when great joy comes... enjoy it!

WEEPING AS JESUS WEPT

"Jesus wept"
(John 11:36)

Just two words from the shortest verse in the Bible and the myth that "real men don't cry" is blown out of the water. Yes, indeed, here we see another side of Jesus' nature - there are things that move Him to tears. Considering that He is the unshakeable Rock and knows all things from the beginning to the end, this is all the more remarkable. Can you picture Him? Jesus with streams of tears flooding down His face – it happened!

Yet we live in a generation that seems to be influenced by two extremes. We have an emotionless hangover from the Victorian era, which refuses to express any sign of affection in public. Then we have the childish sensitivity of the modern era, whereby any little issue can open a floodgate of tears or other emotions. Obviously, neither of these extremes is applicable to Jesus. His outward expressions of emotion were due to inward workings of the Spirit.

Yet much of our emotion is a reflection of the inward stirrings of our flesh rather than of our spirit. As with all physical manifestations, there are two fonts or sources for emotions. Not all tears are "godly tears". We must learn to discern between the two. There are tears from a consecrated heart, but there are tears that come from a selfish, soulful will. One person may be crying because the Lord is touching him deeply but another because of self-pity and remorse. On the outside they look the same, but our responses to them should be different.

We should cry with those who cry godly tears. We empathise with their pain. Yet those who cry selfish tears should be told to dry their eyes and consider their hearts. Self-pity is a font of many tears and is the fruit of envy. The person full of self-pity is one who has compared themselves with others and come away feeling sorry for themselves because they are not as pretty, wealthy, talented (... fill in the adjective). I know someone who weeps at times, as if she had been robbed of her children, and yet really it is all because she is envious of others.

Not all tears are accepted by the Lord. Esau sought the Lord with tears but was rejected because his sorrow was of remorse for losing his blessing rather than repentance for the state of his heart before God. The Bible calls him a "profane person. For you know that afterward, when he wanted to inherit the blessing, he was rejected, for he found no place for repentance, though he sought it diligently with tears". (Heb. 12:16-18).

That said, there are godly tears, and there are things that should move us to such tears. If you aren't moved, then you should cry to the Lord to help you cry! As we read yesterday, there is a "time for weeping" as well as a "time for rejoicing" (Ecc 3:4). So what are these times? Let's consider the times that Jesus wept and what they teach us, for He is the model that we should imitate:

1. Tears reveal compassion

We read in the Gospels that Jesus cried on two separate occasions; firstly, over the fact that his friend Lazarus had died, and secondly, over the apostate city of Jerusalem. When confronted by the loss of a friend to the grave, His heart was touched so deeply that His divine nature responded with tears.

Death, to the heart of God, is a human tragedy. It was never His desire for man. In fact He strictly warned them of the effects of sin (Gen. 2:17). Death is the result of the destructive force of sin. This fact was the reason why Christ came to earth – to overcome death and the grave; to lead captivity captive and to draw the sting out of death itself so that it could be no more (1 Cor. 15:56).

Jeremiah expressed the divine sentiment; "Oh, that my head were waters, And my eyes a fountain of tears, That I might weep day and night For the slain of the daughter of my people!" (Jer. 9:1)

Do you weep at funerals? A friend of mine, years ago, told me that he was not going to be "Italian" and weep at his mother's funeral. How strange! How sad for him to think that weeping was a latino thing to do! A heart that does not express genuine grief is one that will allow inner emotions to build up and explode later like pressure in a volcano. To not cry at your own mother's funeral? How did our culture become so twisted? We should cry at everybody's funeral. Listen to Christ's reaction to other people's anguish and tears; "Therefore, when Jesus saw her weeping, and the Jews who came with her weeping, He groaned in the spirit and was troubled." (John 11.33). Death is devastating! We should be careful too before you rejoice when an evil person dies... the Scripture says that the Lord has no pleasure in the death of the wicked (Ezek. 33:11).

We have misunderstood the heart of our Lord. His heart is tender and loving, not critical and vindictive. We even have prophetic insight into the how Jesus actually died. Was it asphyxiation? Was it blood loss? Look again through the window of Psalm 22:14 "I am poured out like water, And all My bones are out of joint; My heart is like wax; It has melted within Me." Indeed Jesus died of a broken heart – rejected by men, and now, forsaken by God. He loved so much that... it killed Him (John 3:16).

2. Tears reveal concern

The second occasion we read Christ weeping was over Jerusalem. "Now as He drew near, He saw the city and wept over it' (Luke 19:41). This great city had always been at the centre of the move of God for Israel. It was where Abraham had offered Isaac as a sacrifice; where David had brought the ark and where Solomon had built the temple. But now, it had not recognised the hour of its visitation. The same God who had cut covenant with the fathers, was being rejected by the sons. Jesus' tears for them were not tears of rejection like those of a child who had not been invited to a party. Rather He wept at their blindness, their fickleness; how they had fallen into religious rituals rather than relationship with God. He followed His tears with severe warnings about their future. " For days will come upon you when your enemies will build an embankment around you, surround you and close you in on every side, and level you, and your children within you, to the ground; and they will not leave in you one stone upon another, because you did not know the time of your visitation." (Luke 19:43-44)

We read how from His pre-incarnate state God's heart had been rent for the sake of His lost people. "My eyes fail with tears, My heart is troubled" (Lam. 2:11). In this context we understand why the flood of Noah's day was more than rain falling from the sky but tears falling from heaven, for such had become the depravity of the state of the human condition. The Lord warns and disciplines with tears, as a good father does with his children.

Too many people are tearless. When was the last time

you cried? With all the ravages of sin in our world today, it is amazing that we do not cry more. We have become a anesthetised generation. Few things evoke deep compassion in us. There is a more sinister reason as to why so many modern movies are filled with death and violence and the loss of innocence. By having such things screened into our minds on a regular basis we become "accustomed" to them as if they were normal. This is the devil's strategy – to desensitize and thereby deactivate Christians. We don't cry anymore about human tragedies or the loss of loved ones or of innocence. But it is these divine emotions that spur us into action for good.

What moves you - the cry of the poor; the death of the innocent; the eternal damnation of the sinner? Do not any of these bring you to tears? If there is one prayer we should prayer it is "Lord, give us tears; give us compassion!" Have we become so hard-hearted that nothing moves us? We must remember that the ministry of Jesus flowed out of compassion. It was His driving force (Matt. 14:14).

3. Tears move The Father

We know that Hannah, who was barren, received her miracle baby Samuel when she sought God with tears (1 Sam 1:9). There is something about tears that make God the Father particularly interested in our cases. When a parent sees a child weeping, he or she can but lower themselves to the child's level to see if they can put right what is wrong. So too with God; He intervenes with power at times like these.

Interestingly His saving power seems to be dependant on this too. Psalm 126:6 says; "He who continually goes forth weeping, Bearing seed for sowing, Shall doubtless come again with rejoicing, Bringing his sheaves with him." Could it be that an outpouring which will harvest multitudes in our nation has actually been waiting for our tears? I read a story a while back of some of Spurgeon's disciples who had gone out to evangelise a new part of the city and had written to him saying that they had tried everything and failed. He replied to them a two-word response that changed everything: "Try tears!"

SPEAKING AS JESUS SPOKE

And the Word became flesh and dwelt among us, and we beheld His glory, the glory as of the only begotten of the Father, full of grace and truth.
(John 1:14)

One thing that has always amazes me is the response that people had to Jesus' words. Fishermen dropped their nets and followed Him. Prostitutes left their sinful ways and served Him. Tax collectors repented of their extortions and gave their money away. A few words and people would pour out their lives to Him.

What was in these words to the produce such a reaction? They seemed to pierce right to the soul; to shine light in the darkest recesses; and to unlock the meanest heart.

Oh that our words would do the same. It is after all words that conquer hearts. Surely if we can speak the same type of word, people today would be helped in the same kind of way. If His words would become our words, imagine the impact? To our delight we discover that this is the desire of the Holy Spirit – to put His word in our mouths? "The word is near you, in your mouth and in your heart" (Rom 10:8).

Let us consider how we might speak as Jesus spoke:

1. Our words must be full of grace and truth.

Jesus' words were like a sword that pierced into the hearts of His hearers. How did they manage to travel so deep so quickly? The answer is because His words were sharp (not in the sense of harsh and severe, but in the sense of being opposite to blunt). Blunt words bruise. But sharp words slice. Think of the damage a blunt knife does to a piece of meat and, in contrast, how effortlessly a sharp knife slices through. Heb 4:12 tells us that the Word of God is "sharper than any two-edged sword, piercing even to the division of soul and spirit, and of joints and marrow, and is a discerner of the thoughts and intents of the heart."

What then brings this sharpness? Or how can we sharpen our words? The answer is Grace and Truth. These are the two edges that cause God's word to penetrate so deep. If our words are to be like His words, then they too must be filled with both.

Jesus' words were always truthful. He did not pull His punches or tickle people's ears by telling them what they wanted to hear instead of what they needed to hear. His message to the lost multitudes of Israel was "Repent, for the Kingdom of Heaven is at hand" (Mat 3:2). In other words, "rethink your lives, return to the ancient paths, turn around and flee from your sins whilst you can". You can see He wasn't preaching people-pleasing messages. He taught his disciples and followers other things later, after they had step through the door of salvation.

The Bible says that "faithful are the wounds of a faith" (Pro 27:6). A modern translation says, "an honest answer is like a kiss on the lips" (Pro 24:26). Jesus' words always cut to the core. He seemed not to mind whether they were accepted or not, He simply was a "faithful witness" (Rev 1:5).

How honest are your words? Do you speak in order to please your listeners or to please your Heavenly Father? Too many words are seasoned with personal interest. We say things in a certain way because we desire some kind of favour in return. We manipulate through our words! Sadly pulpits are full of such. People flinch from telling the truth for fear of the repercussions.

However, there are those who tell the truth and yet do so in such a self-righteous and condemning manner. They make enemies of sinners rather than friends of them. When they are cut off or persecuted for such, they pride themselves in the fact that they have told the truth. Yet they have missed the key characteristic of the way in which Jesus spoke. Christ did not just speak words of truth but also words of grace. Grace and Truth were like the two sides of a knife's edge that give it is cutting edge. To have one without the other is devastating.

Let us consider this in action. Remember the story in John's Gospel of the woman who is caught in the act of adultery. She was no doubt guilty and Jesus is not one to call black "white" or evil "good" (Psa 38:20). The religious hypocrites asked Jesus want should happen to her. In truth they wanted to either accuse Christ of not obeying their laws or to stone the woman for her sins. They thought it was a win-win situation, whatever option Jesus chose. Yet Jesus response was so extraordinary that it could only have come from a place far higher than the machinations of men's hearts: "He who is without sin among you, let him throw a stone at her first" (John 8:7).

His words pierced so deep into the consciences of the accusers that one be one, from the oldest to the youngest, they dropped their stones and walked away. Why? They realized that they were sinners too (and likely had broken the commandment of adultery). However, Jesus does not stop there. He turns to the woman and says "Woman ... neither do I condemn you. Go and sin no more" (John 8:11). What a perfect combination of truth (don't sin) and grace (I don't condemn you) working together.

The problem with so many people who know and speak the truth is that have little grace. The more truth they know, the more critical and judgmental they become. They have missed the heart of Jesus badly. The more truth you know, the more gracious you should be. The Lord taught this principle in the Sermon on the Mount. After teaching that we should hunger and thirst for righteousness, He then teaches that we should be merciful (Mat 5:6-7). The more righteous you are the more merciful you should be. Yet so often those who go on a moral crusade for righteousness do not add mercy to their message and their manner.

In like manner Grace without Truth has little impact on the heart. As Spurgeon once said, "The message of God's mercy makes no sense outside of the context of the message of His judgment." To speak with grace and not truth is like giving the spoonful of sugar but not adding the medicine. Perhaps this is why so many believers go in and out of church and yet are never healed. The spiritual doctors have been papering over the fundamental issues with slick words and sugary messages. The Lord uses Jeremiah to give stern words to such: "Everyone is given to covetousness;

From the prophet even to the priest.

Everyone deals falsely. For they have healed the hurt of the daughter of My people slightly,

Saying, 'Peace, Peace!'

When there is no peace." (Jer 8:10-11). In this context the word "slightly" means "superficially". Words of grace without truth do not deal with the issue at hand.

Of course the Apostle Paul understood this theme and thereby admonishes the church: "Let your speech always be with grace, seasoned with salt, that you may know how you ought to answer each one" (Col 4:6). That sums it up then. Our speech must always be seasoned with salt. Salt may sting but it preserves life. Our speech must also be with grace. In short the more of God's truth that you know the more gracious, the more patient, the more forgiving you should be of those people who do not follow it.

2. If we have the heart of the Lord, we will have the word of the Lord.

Now this may seem obvious but let us camp here a moment. Whatever came out of the Lord's mouth was an expression of what was in His heart. He spoke His from the core of His being. His words were a revelation of who He was.

So it is with us. "Out of the abundance of the heart the mouth speaks" (Mat 12:34). Whatever is in our hearts, sooner or later comes out of our mouths. This may not happen immediately in communication. We are all quite good at letting people hear what we want them to hear when we first meet. Some people have rehearsed their lines many times over. But as we spend time with others at some stage our hearts will come out on to our sleeves.

This is probably the main reason why so many resist intimate relationships with others in church. They are constantly being invited to join a cell group but always have a reason why they cannot attend. In reality, their pride dominates them to the extent that they fear exposing their weaknesses. They know that if they talk too much people will begin to see who they really are. Now it is wisdom to be reluctant to share your life with those who will and criticize and condemn you. But it is foolish not to share your life with those who are loving and non-judgmental. It is this environment that we all healed and made strong.

To conclude, if we have the heart of the Lord, we will then

speak the razor-sharp word of the Lord. So we must be after His heart as David was in his day. This is not simply a case of memorizing Scripture, though this is vital, but also praying to the Lord to remove the stones from your own heart – those areas of pride and self-will that still exist. Don't assume this happened at your new birth. Yes you have received a new heart (speaking of your spirit), but you still need a new heart (speaking of your soul) – the place of your mind, emotions, character and will. Allow the Lord to put His desires and His character in you and you will see you people all around you become more and more impacted by the words you speak.

D A Y 1 6

SEEING AS JESUS SAW

"His head and hair were white like wool, as white as snow, and His eyes like a flame of fire"
(Rev. 1:14)

To see as Jesus saw we must consider a marvelous and vital characteristic about the vision of the Lord. His eyes did not just receive light, but they gave light. Now let's not get spooky or super-spiritual, but John saw them as eyes of fire in the Book of Revelation. I am not saying that they were like two headlamps on a car in the natural realm but they certainly were in the spiritual realm. He could see things that the people could not see. He could see into people's hearts (Mark 2:8). For this reason He knew people better than they knew themselves. He had a perception of the invisible, spiritual realm because He had eyes that both see, and that give light in order to see.

When we think of our human eyes, we think of them as receptors of light. The light of the sun or artificial light falls upon material matter and reflects into our eyes, thus facilitaing our function within the physical realm. Any human being whose sight is not impaired is able to do this without any difficulty. In this way we are no different from the Lord. When I visited Israel, I stared out across the same blue Galilean sea as He did. I saw the same rocky hills and the same olive groves that have been there for centuries. But this experience, delightful as it was, did not allow me to see as He sees.

To see as Jesus saw is to have "eyes like a flame of fire". It is to be able to throw light upon hidden things as well as receive light from visible things. Jesus taught, "The lamp of the body is the eye. If therefore your eye is good, your whole body will be full of light." (Matt. 6:22). This is why some people read the Scriptures and receive deep understanding and others read them and get nothing. All eyes receive light, but good eyes give light!

Let's consider the main issues here:

1. There are two types of seeing

Jesus operated on a different level from the the world's because of His sight. In His earthly ministry, He was constantly teaching His disciples to see as He saw so that they could do what He had done (John 14:12). We see this happening in the incident of Lazarus' sickness and death. "After that He said to them, 'Our friend Lazarus sleeps, but I go that I may wake him up." Then His disciples said, "Lord, if he sleeps he will get well.' However, Jesus spoke of his death, but they thought that He was speaking about taking rest in sleep. Then Jesus said to them plainly, 'Lazarus is dead.'" (John 11:12-14).

At a glance there seems to be a discrepancy in Jesus' words. Was Lazarus asleep or dead? Did Jesus correct Himself? No; Jesus was trying to correct the disciples. Through His eyes He could see that Lazarus was sleeping in a state of physical death and would be awakened "for the glory of God" (John 11:4). He was uncovering this mystery: that, for believers, physical death is a temporary state from which they will be awoken. Jesus went on to help their understanding with these death-shattering words: "I am the Resurrection and the Life. He who believes in Me, though he may die, he shall live. And whoever lives and believes in Me shall never die (John 11:25-26).

The disciples could not see this at first; after the resurrection things began to be clearer. Later, it is Paul who clarifies the mystery: "But I do not want you to be ignorant, brethren, concerning those who have fallen asleep, lest you sorrow as others who have no hope. For if we believe that Jesus died and rose again, even so God will bring with Him those who sleep in Jesus. (1 Thess. 4:13-14)

Jesus saw things that others didn't. In the country of the Gadarenes, the people saw a mad man who attacked passers-by and deserved to be bound by chains; Jesus saw a human being dreadfully afflicted by a legion of demons - and deserving to be set free (Mark 5:1-17). He could also see how people's minds work and therefore avoided certain situations: " When Jesus perceived that they were about to come and take Him by force to make Him king, He departed again to the mountain by Himself alone (John 16:5). He could see the greed and self-interest in the heart of Judas without necessarily ever having seen him steal from the moneybag (John 12:6). He could see that His ministry would inevitably lead to His death. On numerous occasions He warned His disciples with words such as, "The hour is coming" (John 16:32)

Again, Jesus saw things that others could not see. How about ourselves? Do we see? Do we have these perceptions? Or are we easily beguiled? Do we lack discernment when it comes to choosing into whom we invest our time and energy? Sadly, too often we walk by natural sight rather spiritual sight and suffer the consequences.

2. There is a solution to our blindness

If there was one area that caused Christ's indignation more than any other is was people claiming to see when in reality they were blind. Jesus said to them, "If you were blind, you would have no sin; but now you say, 'We see.' Therefore your sin remains (John 9:41). The Pharisees were called to see and thereby bring light and direction to the people. But because of the selfishness of their hearts they were blind guides leading the blind into the ditch (Luke 6:39). No wonder He confronted them so vehemently! The very leaders who were entrusted to bring God's people into the Promised Land of Heaven were taking them along the broad road to destruction.

Five times in the Gospel of Matthew He chastens the Pharisees by calling them "blind". I quote just one of them: "Blind Pharisee, first cleanse the inside of the cup and dish, that the outside of them may be clean also!" (Matt. 23:26).

Just as Jesus dealt with the Pharisees in His day, so too He had to deal with the church of Laodicea years later: "Because you say, 'I am rich, have become wealthy, and have need of nothing'—and do not know that you are wretched, miserable, poor, blind, and naked" (Rev. 3:16).

The problem exists today. We deceive (blind) ourselves by thinking that we can see more than we can. We have been operating at very low levels of light and have become content with that. Not only are we missing out on being able to see as the Lord can see, but we are too proud to think that we need more light.

The first step towards seeing as Jesus sees is to recognize your own blindness. There is a story of a colony of frogs that lived in the darkness at the bottom of a sewer. One day a young frog falls into the sewer from the world above. He sets about informing the frogs that there is a better, light world above them and that if they worked together they could climb out to be there. However, the other frogs were offended that an outsider, a new-comer, was lecturing them on what was best for the colony, and, when the young frog continued pressing them with his advice, they killed him in order to keep the peace.

No doubt you can see both Jesus and the Pharisees in this story. The story is still relevant today: there is not only a better world above, but also a better world within us now. It is a world of light. A world in which we can begin to truly understand ourselves and the things of this world in the light of God's light. Do not persist in the darkness of mediocrity, religiosity or unbelief! Recognize that you were born to be a child of Light (John 12:36) and cry out to the Lord to open your eyes!

This leads us to the second point: Jesus promises a real solution to those who recognize their blindness. In Revelation 3:17 He counsels us to buy "eye salve, that you may see". There is an ointment that enables us to see. It is, of course, the oil of the Holy Spirit that clears our sight. It is the fire of the Holy Spirit that puts light into our eyes. And yet this ointment is not a gift but rather something that needs to be bought. This is where believers go very wrong. They think that all the things of the Spirit are freely given. Not so; they are something you need to "earnestly desire" (1 Cor. 12:31). In other words, you have to pay a price for them. What currency does the Lord accept for such heavenly merchandise? It is the currency of prayer and faith. For as money 'makes the world go round', prayer and faith make the Kingdom of Heaven go around earth. When we seek the Lord in prayer and ask Him for light He answers from heaven.

Finally, beware of thinking that you have 'arrived'! Paul was given much light; he saw things that even the disciples who had walked with Christ did not see, yet at the end of his life on earth he humbly declared that he was still looking through a dim glass compared to how we will see in the coming Kingdom (1 Cor. 13:12).

Every day, like the Apostle Paul, pray for yourself and for your family and the members of your cell group, that God will open the eyes of our understanding (Eph. 1:18)!.

Suffering as Jesus suffered

"That I may know Him and the power of His resurrection, and the fellowship of His sufferings, being conformed to His death, if, by any means, I may attain to the resurrection from the dead."

(Phil. 3:10-11)

Strange though it may seem, the Apostle Paul's great desire in life was not only to know the Lord and know His power, but also to know His sufferings. Now, most believers want the first two – to know the Person and the Power – but not the Pain! Yet Paul saw that it is through all three things that we are conformed to Christ's death and resurrection life.

The Christian life is, whether you like it or not, a life of suffering and affliction. The early apostles forewarned the young Church: "We must through many tribulations enter the kingdom of God." (Acts 14:22). What was true for Jesus was true for His disciples. He is, of course, the "Captain of salvation, who was made perfect through suffering" (Heb. 2:10). And now, in our turn, we are also "partakers of the sufferings" (2 Cor. 1:7).

Now, immediately, we need to expose a "martyr spirit" that

sometimes rests upon the believer. This person goes about looking to suffer, rather like a masochist goes about looking for pain. There is absolutely no glory in this. It is twisted thinking, and the same mindset that deluded people have who practice flagellation with the belief that, by whipping themselves and causing harm to themselves, they are made more spiritual.

Jesus suffered as and when it was necessary, according to the perfect plan of God. He did not go looking for it. When He did suffer, He did so in the perfect or correct way. There is a reason for our suffering and a right way to respond to suffering. This is the subject of our attention today.

So, let us consider the different types of suffering and the reasons for them:

1. Physical suffering

We all know of Christ's physical suffering on the cross – the whips, the thorns, the nails, the cross. Our minds shudder to think of the physical pain that He went through that day. The agony He must have endured is beyond our personal experience, and we, who flinch at a pinprick in the thumb, are not able to understand the depth of this pain. Each one of us has a cross to carry in his own right (Matt. 16:24). Some crosses are heavier than others; some seem to involve more pain than others. To one is given a life of relative physical ease in a modern, Western nation like ours; to another is given a life of persecution and prison in the East for the same faith. This type of suffering is to be endured meekly, and those who bear lighter loads should offer to help those who suffer greatly to carry their cross.

2. Suffering in the soul

Then, there is the suffering of the soul. These are pains that we experience in the inner man due to circumstances or situations.

They are not physical pains; though a tormented soul will take its toil on the body that carries it. This suffering may include the death of a loved one, the exclusion from or the scorn of society, constant criticism and rejection from unbelieving family members, and, perhaps worst of all, ill-treatment by bosses, spouses, or friends.

The sensation of injustice is one of the heaviest weights to carry in suffering. In these cases you are not suffering for doing evil but for doing good. Your good actions were interpreted badly. At times, goodness is not perceived because of selfishness in the other person's heart. Now this hurts. The Apostle Peter expounds this understanding: "But how is it to your credit if you receive a beating for doing wrong and endure it? But if you suffer for doing good and you endure it, this is commendable before God." (1Pet. 2:20).

There are those workers who are constantly mistreated by their bosses; there are husbands who are held in constant debt by their wives; and, in turn, there are wives who suffer at the hands of over-powering and insensitive husbands. This pain can be long and drawn out over many years, hence its toil on the soul. It threatens to extinguish love like constant dripping of water on a rainy day can put out a fire. The sense of injustice can be very acute, cutting deeper into our hearts than any knife. We want to scream; "This is not fair!" or "I don't deserve this!" and yet, with this type of suffering, we again we must learn to respond as a lamb and not a lion.

3. Sufferings of Christ

There is a deeper suffering yet – that experienced under the weight of burdens of the Lord. Well before Pilate meted out the punishments, Jesus was agonizing in the garden of Gethsemane. Here we find Him imploring His disciples for help: "Then he said to them, My soul is overwhelmed with sorrow to the point of death. Stay here and keep watch with me... Couldn't you men keep watch with me for one hour?" (Matt. 26:38,40).

There was a heavy, heavy, weight being placed on in His soul. So much so that He was keen that His disciples, His friends, would stick with Him and support Him in that dark hour. We know that there in the garden the Father had given Him a cup of poison to drink (Matt. 26:39). The Lord God was putting upon His Son the burden of Sin so that He might become the sacrificial Lamb, which pays the price for others to be forgiven.

In this type of suffering, one must pay a price for another. The Apostles understood this principle and thereby suffered in all ways for the sake of the fledgling Church to which they were giving birth – they were flogged and stoned and imprisoned and eventually martyred in like fashion to their Lord. But again, well before, and well beyond this, they suffered under the hand of the "burdens of the Lord". Paul's heart was constantly rent with anguish for the state of his own people, Israel, to whom the Law was given and yet had hardened their heart against the Messiah (Rom. 9:3). Likewise, the weight of the Church was upon him: "besides the other things, what comes upon me daily: my deep concern for all the churches (2 Cor. 11:28).

There are, therefore, sufferings that you can choose: to take on the burdens of the church in prayer; or to give birth to a church in prayer, through a painful delivery process, as in childbirth; or to labour until Christ is born and then fully formed in the believers (Gal. 4:19). When you do such things you enter the Gethsemane of your world. It is often a dark and difficult experience as you wrestle with the powers of evil to bring forth something new into this world. The suffering here can be intense, the receiving of stripes on your soul can be more painful than the receiving of stripes on your body; for Christ it meant that His sweat became like drops of blood (Luke 22:44). Oh! That the Lord would raise up a generation of radicals who are willing to pay such a price! Truly, this work is only for the overcomers. It is no wonder that Paul was willing to suffer in all these ways for his great desire was, by being conformed into Christ's death, to experience the resurrection life that comes as a result, both now and in the Kingdom to come.

4. Suffering brings perfection

Christ's sufferings were astounding. Yet when faced with physical suffering and the most appalling injustice He was silent, like a lamb before the slaughter (Isa. 53:7). When He faced the burden of being "made Sin" He pressed through in prayer and paid the price for others (2 Cor 5:21). His manner of response is the example we must follow. Do you react at when you are unjustly accused? Do you take on the burdens of others? As you can see, most of us are far from this level of spirituality and must seek the Lord for deep change now.

He read that Christ "was made perfect through suffering'" (Heb. 2:10). How so, since He was already perfect? Christ's perfection was in the fact that His suffering produced His Church. He is the Head and we are the Body. He is now complete or perfect. Suffering causes completion in the Body of Christ. Paul later said, "Now if we are afflicted, it is for your consolation and salvation... I now rejoice in my sufferings for you, and fill up in my flesh what is lacking in the afflictions of Christ, for the sake of His body, which is the church" (1 Cor. 1:5:24).

This is the way the church grows and is perfected, and is the reason that those who pay such a price will receive the glory of the Lord in the great day of reward. Console yourself with these words of Paul and then go and carry your cross gladly: "For I consider that the sufferings of this present time are not worthy to be compared with the glory which shall be revealed in us." (Rom. 8:18)

DAY 18

DESTROYING AS JESUS DESTROYED

For this purpose the Son of God was manifested,
that He might destroy the works of the devil.
(I John 3:8)

Now the word destroy is not a word that God is afraid of using in relation to His Son. For some people, it may offend their religious idea of the Son of God and therefore not enter into their vocabulary, but not so for the Lord. The Lord Jesus came on a seek-out-and-destroy mission to Earth. He defeated the devil's work wherever He found it and then headed deep down into the Mission Control Centre of Satan himself and put a cross, like a sword, right through its centre, causing pandemonium and ripping out its power source.

"Strong words!" you say. Yes, but not my words really; rather, this is just 'modern speak' for Bible narrative. Listen to this: Having disarmed principalities and powers, He made a public spectacle of them, triumphing over them in it." (Col. 2:15)

As mentioned, there is nothing ugly about destroying, if it is the work of evil that we are destroying. This is exactly what Christ did. He came to destroy the 'yoke of bondage'; to destroy death itself; and to destroy the fear of death - all these - by revealing to them resurrection power. In short, Jesus came to take back what the enemy had stolen. He came to destroy the destroyer: "Inasmuch then as the children have partaken of flesh and blood, He Himself likewise shared in the same, that through death He might destroy him who had the power of death, that is, the devil" (Heb. 2:14).

Let us consider today how we might imitate Christ in the destruction of evil:

1. We become equipped for the battle when we see Jesus as a warrior.

We have been looking at Christ from different angles, gazing into this multi-faceted Diamond. Each facet gives us a different glimpse of Him. But as we turn the Diamond we may be surprised to find that He is a destroyer. Some people see Him as Saviour and as Teacher; others realize that He is a Miracle-Worker, Healer and Provider as well; but too few have seen Him as the Destroyer of evil.

When Joshua stood before Jericho's walls he met a man with his sword drawn whom he did not recognize. He asked, "Are you for us or for our enemies?" The man's response revealed that he was indeed the Lord: "Neither, for I come as Captain of the army of heaven" (Joshua 5:13-14). Joshua knew God as a Deliverer, a Healer, and a Provider through the Exodus from Egypt; but he did not know Him as a Warrior, come to destroy and conquer. When Joshua met the Lord in this capacity - as an Warrior Chief, as an Army General, as a Conqueror sent forth to conquer - he then became one as well. He would never have conquered Jericho without this encounter and the transference of this image to himself. Seeing Jesus as the Destroyer of Evil made him a destroyer of evil.

Evil is anything that is contrary to the goodness of God. For this reason King David later said, "I have hated your enemies with perfect hatred" (Ps. 139:22). He had caught the same spirit and, as a picture of Christ, subdued and destroyed the many nations that inhabited and surrounded the land of Canaan. Some people don't understand how the Lord is bellicose. But we need to understand that He is a Destroyer of Evil and a Defender of Good. Hence, when those nations worshipped demon spirits and sacrificed their children to them, the Lord, having warned them to change, raised up Joshua and David and others to destroy them. At first glance it may seem cruel, but, as in the days of Noah's flood, had the Lord not done so, one generation would have polluted the next generation and so on without end.

As any good house cleaner knows, you need to clear up, flush 'loos' and get the trash out of the house, or else it with contaminate everything else.

It is only when we see the Lord in the capacity of a destroyer of evil, that we too become destroyers of evil. It is not enough to know Him as Saviour, Healer and Provider. These things transform you but they do not transform society. We need to know Him as the Overcomer, the Conqueror and the Destroyer of evil.

We live in a pleasure-seeking generation whose desire is to turn the world into a huge amusement park (2 Tim 3:4)! The ethic is: work in order to play. Yet this is a huge, Satanic deception for there is, in reality, a war being waged over the eternal destiny of human beings, and most of those who should know better have been captivated by the razzle-dazzle and neon lights of tinsel-city. We are like the children who get captured by the lollypop man in Chitty-chitty Bang Bang! Modern preaching has been so influenced by this mentality that it stresses pleasures and comfort but rarely addresses war and self-sacrifice. When are we going to wake up and realize that we have not been saved to sit on a luxury-liner but to serve on a battleship?

Oh, that we would see Jesus again today, as Joshua saw Him with a sword drawn in His hand! Then, and only then, will we be able to take back what the enemy has stolen. We would become a new breed of Christian, able to conquer the Jericho's of England.

2. We receive power to fight, when we understand what Jesus has done.

We read of the fact that, in eternity past, Satan, formerly called Lucifer, was thrown out of Heaven along with one third of the angelic forces for trying to usurp the throne. It was a total defeat. For divine reasons he and the other fallen angels were cast to the earth, the place of habitation for God's creation, Mankind. Without going into a long Bible study, let me cut to the point of our study today. Satan does not war directly against God any longer; this is, after all, a one-sided battle, and he would be sure to lose. Rather, he wars against Man in order to get at God and to retain his control of this realm.

Jesus became a man to be the Captain of the Army of Earth in order to cast Satan from the earth, as he has already been cast from Heaven. Jesus, the second Adam, came to do what the first Adam had not done. Adam was seduced into the serpent's mouth through temptation and then bitten with the poisonous sting of sin. This killed him, spiritually at first and later, physically. Jesus came to draw out the poison from the serpent by having all sin placed upon Himself on the cross at Calvary, for the sting of death is sin (1 Cor. 15:56). Hence the serpent has no sting any more. He can still deceive and control people through fear, just as a non-venomous snake will cause people who cannot recognize her skin pattern to panic and fear. But the fact of the matter is that death no longer has its sting; Satan's power has been stripped from him; he is a defeated foe, waiting for the judgment of everlasting fire. He is a lion without his teeth and claws, a snake without a bite. Whilst physical death still exists today, that too will be destroyed in the end (1 Cor. 15:26).

Jesus combatted Satan at every point of His ministry, from the temptations in the wilderness to His sufferings on the cross. It was arm to arm combat, swords drawn in spiritual fight. Jesus had destroyed strongholds in people's minds, cast demons out of the oppressed and healed people from spirits of infirmity. Then, in a final act in the destruction of evil, He gave his life at Calvary, descended in spirit to the prisons of Hades and from there led the most glorious liberation of captives that history has ever known - destroying the demonic powers in the process. He arose as the Firstborn from the dead, followed by a procession of saints who had died in times past, and returned to His disciples giving them the power and authority "to trample on serpents and scorpions and over all the power of the enemy." (Luke 10:19)

Now, the believer is equipped to destroy the devil's work too. Jesus said, "In My name they will cast out demons; they will speak with new tongues; they will take up serpents; and if they drink anything deadly, it will by no means hurt them; they will lay hands on the sick, and they will recover." (Mark 16:17-18)

3. We will win the war of our time, if we awake from our slumber.

Delilah's strategy to overcome Samson was to lull him to sleep on her lap with sweet kisses and lullaby songs. By doing so, she put to sleep the hope of Israel and robbed him of his strength. Satan's strategy against us, the Church today, is the same. Many believers have been lulled to sleep and taken out of the game. Our prayers to the Lord, if we pray at all, are like a shopping list for Santa rather than intercessions to set men free.

Jesus was a man with a sword drawn. Not a physical one in His hand, but a spiritual one coming out of His mouth. For the Word of God is the Sword of the Spirit (Eph. 6:17). His words broke the chains off people's backs; His words set the demon-possessed free; His words destroyed the fear of death and shattered false ideologies that held the people in darkness.

Have you heard the story of His imitator, Paul, in the book of Acts? It reads like a war journal! This man took it upon himself to take up 'arms' and destroy the false gods of the era. Remember, please, that his battle was not against people. No, but against the powers and principalities that had blinded the people with their lies. His weapons of warfare were prayer and preaching. He was unafraid to march into the enemy's camp, in Rome or Ephesus or Athens, and to take on the foreign gods and their advocates and earnestly persuade them about the things of God (Acts 19:26). To persuade is not just to present your case, it is to then destroy any rebuttals that come as a result. Whole cities were turned upside down because of this warrior for the Lord.

Oh! Where, oh where, are such men today? In our generation of political correctness we have disengaged from the fight for men's souls! Do you not know that, unless the truth is spoken, all will believe a lie? Unless the light shines, all will sit in darkness. "But", you say; "It may cost me my job, my reputation, my friends, my life!" Yes, indeed, it might. He who fears sacrifice is not apt for war. Many mighty warriors for the Lord, who have gone before us, sealed their testimonies with their own blood. It cost them everything, but the prize was worth the price. That is why Jesus endured the cross and suffered the shame. He knew about the victory that would follow – the gates of Heaven open and multitudes of people flooding in from every nation, tribe and tongue.

It is time to decide what type of believer you want to be – a soldier or a sucker, a warrior or a wimp! Tough words, yes – like the word "destroy"; but I've discovered something - to be an overcomer is not for the faint-hearted.

BUILDING AS JESUS BUILT

"And I also say to you that you are Peter, and on this rock I will build My church"
(Mat 16:18)

Have you ever seen Jesus in this way – a builder? Whilst we can't quite imagine Him in jeans and a hard hat, the truth is that throughout His earthly ministry He was laying the foundation of a building that would house the presence of God. Let me back up so that you can see this more clearly, because understanding this issue will, I hope, change the way you act for the rest of your life.

In Matthew 16:18 we read that Jesus is building His Church. The purpose for all His ministerial work and even His sacrificial death is revealed here. He is saying, 'I am doing all this in order to build something for my Father'. Think of it like a son gathering materials and working all day in order to make a precious gift for his father. The hard work was for a purpose.

Just as Moses built the tabernacle in the wilderness according the pattern that he had seen on the mountain, and Solomon built the Temple according to his father David's desire, so too Jesus was building a house according to the desire and the pattern of His heavenly Father. This new house was to be made not of canvas or stone, but of "living stones", or, in other words, of believers. Each person who comes to Christ is to be part of this living edifice. It is the most beautiful work that eyes will ever see.

Some people dedicate their lives to winning souls on the street. This is admirable but it is not all that the Lord has called us to do. Others have specialist ministries in areas such as finance, healing, relationships and our need to honour Israel; but, again, the will of the Lord is that, whilst these are vital, we do much more than this. Just as He is both part of the building (the Foundation), and also its builder, so too He has called us to be both part of the building (the edifice) and also its builder.

Jesus said to Peter that He was going to build His church through him. It is not Peter who will be doing the building; rather it is the Lord in him and through him. The work of the Holy Spirit on earth is to build the Church through us. We are not able to do this in our own strength and ability. It is the work of the anointing in us and through us. "For unless the Lord builds the house, they labour in vain who build it" (Ps. 127:1). Believers who never pray are people who build in their own strength. Their labour is in vain and will have no eternal value.

There are others who labour in vain because they are busy doing things for the Lord that have nothing to do with building Him a house. They seem to think that anything done in His name is acceptable. Not so! The only thing Jesus is doing is building His Church. Best to hook up with His plans rather than think He will join you in yours! There are others, too, who have a very limited vision and think that have fulfilled the call of God on their lives by being worshippers or intercessors or administrators. Actually, you have been called to much more than this. You have been called to be a builder of something that is glorious and everlasting. This may mean you have to change your plans for the rest of your life.

Let us have a look at the main responsibilities of a builder:

1. The builder starts with a plan.

Before we start building, we should be sure that we know what to build. Jesus, of course, is the expressed desire of God. The Lord wants to build a habitation for His presence, which He can fill with His glory. This amazing place is called in Scripture "My church".

He has revealed His desire to faithful servants over the centuries. He asked Moses to make Him a tabernacle. David then discovered that the Lord wanted a house. Jesus laid the foundation stone and laid down the twelve apostles as His supporting stones. Paul was the chief architect who then gave direction for all the Church over the ensuing centuries to build in the correct way until Christ's glorious return when He will "put the roof" upon the building and fill it with His glory.

The tragedy is that so few people seem to have seen or understood the plan. At a basic level there are those who think that a church is bricks and mortar and not people. Then there are church leaders who teach that to serve God you need only to stop sinning and otherwise do whatever you like in the name of the Lord. Also, there are believers who busy themselves with good works, even ministry projects, but never build the Church.

It is time for all to put down their tools for a moment and consider what the Lord's plan is and not their own.

2. The builder gathers materials.

The first thing a builder does is to gather the materials to work with. Stocks of limestone where hewn from local rock to build the

Temple of the Lord. In the new temple God uses "living stones", for His Church is not a building of stone but a community of covenant people (1 Pet. 2:4). Every believer is called to be part of the building, for we are the "temple of the Holy Spirit" (1 Cor. 3:16).

As the Temple builders cut away blocks of stone from the local limestone bedrock, so today the Lord separates people to Himself from each nation. There is a calling out and a cutting away process that happens when a person converts. When the Lord calls a person, his purpose changes. By being attached to the Lord, he becomes detached from the world. Often, this means that he detaches himself from his old friends, or even family members, and the places he used to visit and the things he would do. For this reason Jesus said He did not come to bring peace but a sword. He said, "For I have come to set a man against his father, a daughter against her mother, and a daughter-in-law against her mother-in-law" (Matt. 10:34). A person needs to do this so that his new life is not hindered by soulish ties or bad habits.

"Simon Peter answered and said, 'You are the Christ, the Son of the living God.' Jesus answered and said to him, 'Blessed are you, Simon Bar-Jonah, for flesh and blood has not revealed this to you, but My Father who is in heaven. And I also say to you that you are Peter and on this rock I will build My church.'" (Matt. 16:18)

Some have thought that Peter is here being elevated into a special position above the other apostles to be the head of the Church. However, the words "this rock" do not refer to Peter but rather to the revelation that Peter had that Jesus is the son of God. When you have revelation of the person and plan of God you become a rock that Christ can build with.

Later, Peter was not only a rock that Christ could build upon, but also a builder that could be used to bring in other rocks too for the building of God's Church. "Be saved from this perverse generation." (Acts 2:40).

3. The builder prepares his materials.

But gathering materials is not enough. The materials must be of the right quality. At inception, the stones that the Lord chooses are not fit for His purposes. Since human beings are fallen, the Lord has to transform His people into those having the right qualities and consistency. We are saved in spirit when we are born again. Now the salvation process needs to affect our souls. This is what produces the transformation necessary for people to be used by God.

He finds us in a common state, just as coal is common in the earth and sand is common in the sea. Yet, through the process of transformation, He turns the common into the precious. The New Jerusalem is not built with bricks and mortar, nor even common stone, but with precious stones. In fact, the Scripture says that only gold, silver and precious stones are used in this building (1 Cor. 3:11). For this reason, the Lord must transform us, individually, in order to be fit for use. Charcoal, whilst a common element, is transformed into a diamond through the use of extreme heat and high pressure. In the same way, the Lord transforms His people through the fire of the Holy Spirit and the pressure of the tests and trials that He allows them to face. It is like when a single grain of sand enters an oyster; the oyster secretes a substance around the sand that, over time, forms a pearl. In this way, a common, ordinary piece of sand is transformed into a precious pearl.

There is good news for those of us who start out like Peter, the fisherman from Galilee, with all his imperfections, brashness, lack of insight and fears: he does not finish the same way. In fact, in the New Jerusalem he is one of the great pearls that are the gates to the city. He and the other apostles are those who have laid down the doctrine of salvation so that others can enter in.

This shows us that if we are to be builders we must do more that win people for Christ; we must also help the converts to be transformed. The quality of the material determines the level of their use. The best materials in a building are used in the most prominent positions. The materials with the greatest consistency are used as pillars and support walls. These carry the weight of the building but also stand out most. Leaders are those who are consistent and can support weight. This is your calling.

4. The builder places the materials together correctly.

Building sites are messy and ugly environments. Why? Because the materials have yet to be put in the right positions. Until a stone is its place, it is not fulfilling its purpose. The building remains a pile of bricks. As soon as the stone is put in the wall it is has fulfilled its purpose.

So many Christians are like a brick in a pile! They may be a beautiful brick because they have now been transformed, but they never fulfill their prophetic purpose because they are not part of the building. They are part of the Church in name but not in practice. There are many believers today who are "doing church" at home, separating themselves from the Body. Others are serving in para-church organisations and feel that they are fulfilling God's purpose, but they never become part of the local church. They busy themselves with their good works; they pride themselves that they have led someone to the Lord or had someone healed but they don't build a building for the Lord. They have, at best, a very limited vision of the Lord's plan, and, at worst, a pride that makes them feel superior to being part of a local church.

When you put a building block in a wall, it will rest upon

those below and then support those above it. In this way a wall is built. So too the Church! Each of us has leaders who have gone before us and upon whom we rest. Each of us too will have new believers placed upon us, needing our support. This is how the Lord builds His Church. This Church is His glorious, eternal desire. It is to be His resting place forever – are you in, or are you out? It is time to put on a new hat – a hard hat, for this is serious work – and become a builder.

DAY 20

Submitting as Jesus submitted

Then He went down with them and came to Nazareth, and was subject to them, but His mother kept all these things in her heart. And Jesus increased in wisdom and stature, and in favor with God and men.

(Luke 2:51)

Throughout the Bible a principle emerges that authority is given to those who are under authority. We see this in the life of Christ from an early age. It is no coincidence that He increased in wisdom and stature and favour because He had chosen to submit to His parents. Submission is the key to advancement in the Kingdom of God. Many Christians never experience favour with God and man, and the authority that comes with it, because they have never learned to submit as Christ did. They think that leaders teach on submission in order to get everybody to obey them. They have yet to see that they are the ones who gain from submission, for it deals with the human ego (which is at enmity with God) and it puts the believer in a position where he can be promoted by God.

To submit is to be subject to or in obedience to the will of another. Submission is to come under the mission of another. Yet there are so many people who have never really done this. They always want to be the visionary, the top dog, the one in control. They have never really learned to serve another with all of their heart or to think that someone else could have more revelation and wisdom than them. They have the "Adam" complex and feel that everything that God does on planet earth should always start with them. Therefore they negate other "moves of God" as not genuine, and criticise other preachers as "deceiving the masses". Yet by doing so they are destroying the future that they could have. Favour, wisdom, stature are given to those who submit to the authority figures in their lives.

Jesus' authority is extraordinary. The natural mind boggles to the fact that all creation obeys His commands. We tend to think this is because of some special gifting on His life. We have not seen that this actually is a result of His submissive spirit.

We read of the wind and the water obeying His command: "So the men marveled, saying, "Who can this be, that even the winds and the sea obey Him?" (Mark 8:27). We read of the demonic realm being subject to His word - "For with authority He commands even the unclean spirits, and they obey Him." (Mark 1:27). We also read of people obeying His commands over and above the commands and customs of the powers that were in that day - "But Peter and the other apostles answered and said: "We ought to obey God rather than men." (Acts 5:29).

The reason why the spiritual and material realm obeyed His word is the fact that He obeyed the authority figures in His life. Now everybody wants to have authority but few people want to be under authority. It smacks against the pride of man, which is why so many resist it. But by doing so, God resists them and withdraws His favour and grace. Hence they live their lives complaining that they are not recognized or released; but, in reality, it is because they do not have a submissive spirit. We need to go to Christ and learn to be like the one who is "gentle and lowly of heart" (Mat 11:29) if we want to have the authority that He had.

Let us consider then this principle in Jesus' life:

1. Jesus submitted to His natural father

We catch a glimpse into Jesus' childhood with the amazing account of His visit to the temple at Jerusalem at the age of twelve. The story is well known. At the end of the feast the touring party from Galilee, returns home and Jesus' father and mother assume that He is travelling with relations with the group. Only later do they discover that He is not among them and hurry back to Jerusalem to find Him sitting at the feet of the temple elders, completely unperturbed, conversing with them about the things of God. When asked by his anxious mother what He was doing He gave a seemingly dismissive reply; "Did you not know that I must be about My Father's business" (Luk 2:50).

Here Jesus is clearly stating His priorities: that God is His real Father and that God's business is His real business. This is a lesson that every parent should understand: our children belong to the Lord, not to us, and they were created for God's business not man's. But the story does not end there. The narrative continues. "Then He went down with them and came to Nazareth, and was subject to them". (Luk 2:51).

Even though God was His "true" Father, He still submitted to Joseph and Mary. The Fifth Commandment is to "Honor your father and your mother, that your days may be long upon the land which the Lord your God is giving you." (Exo 20:12). Paul later explains that "this is the first commandment with promise: "that it may be well with you and you may live long on the earth." Now this is favour - long life and things being well with you. These are not trivial things. So many people suffer throughout their lives and even die before their time because they do not fulfill this command.

Jesus was the Son of God, and thereby He knew so much more than His parents. He knew more than the teachers in the temple, let alone his father Joseph who was a tradesman. Nonetheless He subjected Himself to their authority, their wisdom and their control. How many young people of today, even though their character and wisdom is nowhere close to that of Jesus at the same age, rile and rage against their parents and assume that they have nothing to teach them? You should honour your parents not because of their perfection but because of their position. To dishonor your parents is to invite a future full of problems, heartaches and disappointments.

2. Jesus submitted to His "spiritual" father

I use the term "spiritual father" with care here, but please follow the point. Every spiritual son has a spiritual father - a person who nurtures him in the ways of the Lord. The Bible is full of such relationships - Elisha was to Elijah, Paul was to Timothy, Aquila and Priscilla were to Apollos; to name but a few.

John the Baptist was the "senior" prophet at the time of our Lord's upbringing. Jesus Himself said that John had come in the same spirit of the great prophet Elijah and that He was greatest of all the prophets (Luk 1:17). Yet, at the same time, even the "least in the Kingdom of God is greater than he" (Luke 7:28). If the least in the Kingdom was greater than He, imagine how much greater the King of that Kingdom was greater.

Jesus was a far "superior" prophet and yet He submitted to John. When He went to be baptized by John at the river Jordan, John said to Him that it should have been the other way around. Jesus should be baptizing John. However, Jesus replied that he should "permit it to be so ... in order to fulfill all righteousness"

(Mat 3:15). We learn here that our righteousness becomes complete when we submit to our spiritual elders. It is interesting to note that the moment of His submission to John at the river Jordan was the moment that He began His ministry in which diseases and demons were subject to His word. Authority comes to those who are under authority.

Yet how many believers submit to no one? They are laws to themselves. They do what they want to do, when they want to do it, and are answerable to no one. They always seem to be out of sink with the rest of the church. When it is time to fast they want to feast; when it is time to pray they want to read their bibles; when it is time to teach the believers, they want to be on the streets evangelizing. They don't recognize any one as a "spiritual father" in their lives; they hate to call a man "pastor" because that means they have to honour someone else instead of have the honour themselves. No wonder that they have little authority. No wonder they become like lone islands in the sea. They might make a whole lot of noise but they have no clout.

In comparison, the "spiritual son" who recognizes his "spiritual fathers", will always rise to the heights because he is standing on the shoulders of others who have gone before him and building on the wisdom that has been passed down to him.

3. Jesus submitted to His heavenly Father

Finally we know that Jesus subjected Himself to His Father. His delight was to do God's will (Psa 40:8). The crunch moment came at the beginning of His sufferings in Gethsemane when it seemed that the will of the Father and the will of the Son were opposed: "O My Father, if it is possible, let this cup pass from Me; nevertheless, not as I will, but as You will." (Mat 26:39).

Yet even in the face of physical and spiritual suffering to a degree that we can hardly imagine, He subjected Himself to

God's best for His life: "Into your hands I commit my spirit" (Luk 23:46). How many of us resist God's dealings in our lives? We buck the cross that He puts on our backs. We are sweet as pie when we our wills are aligned with His but react like spoilt children when His will and our will collide!

The secret to Christ's authority was His submission. This made Him a channel God could use. We all have an anointing for great purposes; we all have been called to do great and mighty things; yet ultimately only those who learn to submit will ever achieve such.

Discipling as Jesus discipled

So then, after the Lord had spoken to them,
He was received up into heaven, and sat down at
the right hand of God.
(Mark 16:19)

This is an appropriate place to finish the 21-day study of Imitating Jesus; for, in a sense, Jesus' earthly ministry was only complete once His disciples were prepared to take on the work that He had started. If you think about it, the Lord did not need to stay on earth for forty days after His resurrection and before His ascension. He could have made a quick appearance and then risen up to heaven to take His rightful place at the side of His Father. So why the "delay"? It is clear from Scripture that there was still some discipleship that needed to take place before He could delegate to His team and "say goodbye". The doubters, such as Thomas, needed Him to give them infallible proofs of His conquest of death so that their unbelief was defeated once and for all. The fearful, such as Peter, needed to be restored and forgiven for their weaknesses. The unclear, such as all the twelve, needed further briefings on the Kingdom of God .... and much more, before He departed. As the Scripture above says, He was received up into heaven after He had spoken to them.

If there is one thing that every Christian minister should have in his or her mind from the outset of their ministry it is this: Your disciples are your legacy. The strength of the disciple determines the future of the cause. Jesus had taken lumps of coal (as we saw in a previous study) and turned them into rocks of diamonds. When His preparation work was completed, He left.

There is something deeply touching about the ascension to heaven. Like a farewell to a friend at a train station or a tearful goodbye at the airport, loved ones had gathered to hug and kiss and say their goodbyes their Lord, their "beloved". No doubt their minds were racing so fast and their hearts beating so strongly that afterwards they must have had to shake themselves from thinking it was a dream. But here they were, on the Mount of Olives, overlooking Jerusalem, a short walk from Calvary, with the God of the Universe. He spoke to them as a pastor and as a father, as a brother and a friend, and as a commissioner and a captain.

This was no simple "Goodbye! We hope to see you again". It was the last words of the Commander of the host of heaven as to the plans of God for the world: "Wait in Jerusalem until you receive the promise of My Father... After you have received power you will be my witnesses ... to the ends of the earth." (Luke 24:49; Act 1:8) This was no longer a disparate, disjointed gang of unskilled men but a trained unit of darkness-destroyers and Kingdom-builders! The disciples were to head down the hill and get clothed in the battle-suit of the Holy Spirit.

So how then did Jesus disciple these men? How did such profound change happen in their lives? Whilst this is a huge topic, let us consider some main features of discipleship. We should always remember to make discipleship our passion and our priority... it is indeed the only legacy we will have on earth, and our crown and glory in heaven. Paul called his disciples: "my beloved and longed-for brethren, my joy and crown" (Phil. 4:1).

1. Jesus taught His disciples

The main thing that Jesus did for His disciples was to teach them. Yes, they walked together and ate together and ministered together, but His main commission was to teach them. This is how He served them. This is how He equipped them. Whereas He preached to the multitudes, He would take His disciples aside and teach them personally about the Kingdom of God. He taught them what a faithful steward looked like, in the Parable of the Talents, and they became faithful stewards. He taught them the power of persistency through the parable of the persistent widow, and they became determined in prayer.

Herein we find a principle: You get what you preach for. You reap what you sow. The Word of God will take root in the hearts of your disciples and grow into a mighty tree of abundant blessing and spiritual fruit within them.

Teaching was always Jesus' priority for His disciples. When an incident happened on the way, Jesus would often use it to teach. The religious hypocrites would dispute with Him, so He immediately gave warnings and teaching on the leaven of the Pharisees (Matt. 16:6). Jesus served His disciples by teaching them. Many people think that the true picture of a servant is someone who sweeps the floors or prepares food and cleans up. Yet we never read about Jesus doing these menial tasks -although He was the greatest servant of all. It is not that this is wrong, and someone does need to clean the floor, but Jesus served by teaching because, over and above everything, this was what the disciples needed – not the bread of earth but the bread of heaven. For this reason He did not rebuke Mary, even though her sister Martha complained that she was doing all the hard work whilst Mary simply sat and listened to Him. He said that Mary, not Martha, had chosen the "good part" (Luke10:42).

How much do you teach your disciples? How much do you truly invest your wisdom into others? There are many who like to "hang out together" and eat pizzas or watch movies together. But what about teaching them and walking with them through ministry issues?

2. Jesus exhorted His disciples

Jesus was never afraid to address issues in His disciples. Just after He had commended Peter for hearing from heaven, He then rebuked him for hearing from hell. In the first moment Peter had heard God the Father speak into his heart that Jesus was the "Son of the Living God" (Matt. 16:16). In the second moment Peter had been influenced by Satan to urge Jesus not to follow God's will. This resulted in Jesus saying to Peter, "Get behind Me, Satan! You are an offense to Me, for you are not mindful of the things of God, but the things of men." (Matt. 16:23).

There is a difference between a disciple-maker and a friend. A friend will not necessarily point out your weaknesses. If he does he might lose your friendship; therefore he often choses not to. We all retain friends in this way. But a disciple-maker must point out the weaknesses. It is his role and responsibility. If the disciple cannot see his own impudence or lack of spirituality, then, for his own sake, he needs a brother who has more light to point it out in love.

Jesus was this type of leader – not a mere encourager but an exhorter too. Evidently, His motive was always Love. He confronted spiritual blindness in people because He did not want them to end up in the ditch or lead anybody else there. The reason why so few leaders exhort others in this manner is that they are afraid of loosing them. I have learned this. If you compromise to get someone, you will have to compromise to keep them, and if you do this, they will always remain a 'thorn in your flesh'. As a father corrects a son for his own good, so a disciple-maker must correct his disciples for their good. No one ever reaches the top of their game unless they have a coach that points out the bad as well as the good.

I sometimes wonder how people can be believers for so long and change so little! Their negative habits or childish characteristics are still there years later. Jesus turned His team around in three short years. Why the difference? Many believers have never been truly discipled. They have lacked father figures in their lives who want to invest in them rather than lord over them. Then there are others who have never opened themselves up to correction. If you want to be wise you should have a different attitude. If you had the chance of having personal coaching from a millionaire, you perhaps would say; "Please tell me everything I am doing wrong, so that I can also become a millionaire too". However, we, foolishly, seem to be reluctant to open up our lives to disciple-makers who could help us to receive the riches of the Kingdom of Heaven.

There are always those who don't want to receive instruction or correction. One of the most tragic stories in Scripture is that of the rich young ruler who refused to give up his love of money and become a disciple of Christ (Matt. 19:16). With these people, before long, your words of advice become 'pearls before swine' (Matt. 7:6). They don't give you space to speak into their lives, even though they may sit in your pews. If you push them at all, they flee.

Jesus was never afraid of loosing people. He said what needed to be said with words that mixed grace with truth. Many did turn back. But for His true disciples it was a great honour to be under His tutelage. Remember, they had not chosen Christ -rather He had chosen them.

3. Jesus modeled things for His disciples

One of the best ways to transfer your anointing, your passion, and your purpose to others is to model it for them. When they see you do things then they learn how to do them themselves. We say that a picture speaks a thousand words. More than this, a model showing you how to do something can be better than a library of words.

The disciples learned to preach as He had preached, heal as He had healed, shepherd as He had shepherded, give as He had given, love as He had loved, and die as He had died… so that they might live as He had lived!

This very thought has been the purpose of this 21-day prayer and study campaign: that we might become imitators of Christ. We could never have had a better model. He is the express image of God, and He showed us how to do everything that He has asked us to do. As we look at Jesus, we become like Him. Even today we have His Holy Spirit with us to bring to our remembrance all that He did and taught (John 14:26). Imitating could never have been better; imitating could never have been easier - for He lives within us to will and do His purposes.

It is upon this note that I would like to finish. Our imitation of Him is not something contrived or forced. It is not a drummed up attempt by our flesh to copy Him. If it were so, we would all fail miserably. But the good news is, it is the Holy Spirit in us who gives us the power to be like Jesus. When we let go and let Him loose within us, we find that it is the Spirit's desire and delight to conform us into the image of Christ. I urge you to enjoy the process. Today you look more like Christ than you did yesterday.

Because of this I can say with confidence… you future looks really bright!

"The Lord bless you and keep you; The Lord make His face shine upon you,

And be gracious to you; The Lord lift up His countenance upon you,

And give you peace." (Num 6:24-26)

Other books by Giles Stevens:

The 11th Question
The spiritual self-evaluation test.

The best-selling outreach tool that helps believers share their faith with friends and families through a self-evaluation test. The premise of this book is that people only drink medicine (material or spiritual) when they first know that they are sick.

Winning Your World
How to be fruitful in a barren land

Apply the principles of this book to any area of life and see new life and growth appear as a result. In particular Giles' shareswisdom in the area of being more fruitful soul-winners. The premise of the book is that the difference between successful and unsuccessful fisherman is that the former know more than later.

For more information & materials, please contact us:
The Vine Studio
5 Blackworth Court
Highworth, SN6 7NS
01793 862 224
https://www.facebook.com/vinechurchuk
www.vinechurch.co.uk
admin@vinechurch.co.uk